Pc

Political Savvy

Systematic Approaches to Leadership Behind-the-Scenes

Joel R. DeLuca, Ph.D.

Evergreen Business Group
Berwyn, Pennsylvania 19312

EBG Publications
Berwyn, Pennsylvania 19312

This publication was designed to provide accurate and authoritative information on the subject matter covered. It is published with the understanding that neither the author nor the publisher is engaged in rendering legal or accounting services. If legal advice or other expert assistance is required, the service of a competent professional should be sought.

© 1999 by EBG Publications. All rights reserved.

Library of Congress Cataloging-in-Publication Data
Political Savvy: systematic approaches to leadership behind-the-scenes / Joel R. DeLuca.
   p. cm.
Includes bibliographical references and index.
   ISBN: 978-0-9667636-1-4 (paperback)
   ISBN: 0-9667636-0-2 (hardcover)
   1. Office politics. 2. Leadership. 1. Title.
   HF5386.5.D45 1992
   658.4'09—dc20   91-33528
                                  CIP

   Printed on acid-free paper.
Manufactured in the United States of America.

Dedication

To the legions of unheralded individuals who, though often resisted by the very organizations they're trying to help, continue working at leadership behind-the-scenes.

To Kurt Lewin. I hope he would have smiled at this type of book.

Contents

List of Exhibits..ix
Preface to the 2nd Edition.............................xi
Preface to the 1st Edition.............................xiii
Acknowledgments......................................xix

Part One
Choosing to Become an Active, Ethical Player

1   Introduction.....................................3
2   Understanding Your Own Political Style..........7
3   The Political Blind Spot........................27

Part Two
Systematically Understanding the Political Lay of the Land

4   A Case Example: The Future of the Milford Steel Company..................................53
5   Mapping the Political Territory: The OPMT Tool . 63

Part Three
Taking Action: Strategy Formulation

6   Developing Coalitions..........................83
7   Charting a Political Strategy: Agenda Linking....95

Part Four
Tactics and Techniques of the Politically Savvy

8   101 Ways to Shoot Oneself in the Foot: Know the Organization's Culture 119

9	Building Momentum	127
10	Customizing Attempts at Influence	153
11	Handling the Machs	185

Part Five
Summary and Conclusions

| 12 | Summary | 203 |
| 13 | Conclusions | 213 |

Sources for Epigraphs & Exhibits ... 219
Further Readings ... 223
Index ... 231

List of Exhibits

1   Popular Beliefs about Organization Politics 8
2   The Political Style Grid 11
3   The Political Blind Spot 27
4   A Perspective on Power 29
5   Influence Continuum 31
6   Manipulation versus Ethical Influence Guide 32
7   Ethical Situations 32
8   Abraham Lincoln Quote 33
9   Excerpt from an Interview with Sir Brian Urquart 35
10 Rationalist and Savvy Perspectives
    on Organizations 36
11 A Rationalist's Dream 37
12 Journey from Novice to Master Manager 40
13 Interest Grid................................... 41
14 Organization Politics 43
15 Machiavellian versus Savvy Distinctions 45
16 Characteristics of Politically Savvy Individuals .. 49
17 OPMT—Five Basic Questions Sheet (sample) 64
18 OPMT—The Political Data Sheet (sample) 65
19 OPMT—Organization Politics Map (sample)..... 66
20 OPMT—The Political Data Sheet:
    The Chromium Project........................... 69
21 OPMT—Organization Politics Map:
           The Chromium Project................... 71
22 Complex Organization Politics Map 77
23 "Ha! Webster's blown...," by Gary Larson 79
24 Excerpt from Niccolo Machiavelli's The Prince ... 84
25 "There are no great men ...," by Chas Addams .. 88
26 The Chromium Project: Agendas Summary 97
27 OPMT—Organization Politics Map:
           The Chromium Project 105
28 Political Savvy Definition 112

29	"Attaaaaaaack!" by Gary Larson	120
30	Avoiding Shooting Oneself in the Foot	121
31	The 51 Percent Guide	128
32	"No" ..."He said no" ..."Said no," by Ziegler	129
33	Use of Group Settings	134
34	The Many-Few-Many-Few Technique	148
35	Executive Attention	154
36	An Aspect of Executive Attention	155
37	Levels of Involvement	163
38	Plan-Act Matrix	169
39	On-the-Spot Face-Saving	176
40	The Two-Shots-Then-Salute Technique	177
41	A Long-Term Perspective	181
42	Confronting a Mach	187
43	How They Catch Monkeys in Malaysia	193
44	Developmental Staircase	216

Preface to the Second Edition

When I asked people who read the book's first edition how I should best go about revising it for the second edition, the primary response was to leave it alone. So for the most part that is what I've done. I did correct some obvious errors and misprints that various readers were kind enough to point out. I also removed some material that readers found more confusing than helpful. Some were in favor of adding examples from specific corporations, as is popular in management books. But most commentators felt the issues and examples used were timeless enough that the book stood well enough on its own without them. I also reduced the price of the book to make it more affordable.

A lot has happened since the book came out in 1992. Although it received very little marketing, word of mouth and seminars based upon the book have sold out the first edition. Seminars have been given in almost every major city in the United States, and several countries abroad, thanks primarily to the Institute for Management Studies. IMS is an organization which has promoted it continuously over the last three years. As a result the book and seminar have been used in a wide spectrum of organizations from Bell Atlantic to Victoria Secret, to the FBI. As I had hoped, the political savvy side of leadership seems as valuable in public sector organizations as in private sector ones.

Perhaps the most gratifying letters I have received are from professionals and managers who were becoming very frustrated with the politics in their organizations and were beginning to give up and become cynics regarding initiating change. Reading the book helped them rekindle their spark and instilled hope that they could still make significant contributions in their firms. I was also pleased by the letters in the vein of "I wish I had these concepts and tools earlier in my career so I could have made more of a difference". Along this vein were comments from those that expressed the value of the book in coaching and mentoring others.

One somewhat unexpected theme in much of the feedback was regarding the issue of ethics. These comments basically stated that if they had known that ethics was going to be so integral to the book, they probably never would have read it because of the "preachiness" often associated with the topic. However, since the ethical nature of the truly politically savvy is embedded in action and achieving concrete results, they then reported gaining a better sense of the practical business and career benefits of an ethical orientation.

One of the exciting trends that the book seems to be striking a chord with is what I'll call, entrepreneurial leadership. As downsizing shrinks organizations, as information technology creates opportunities for more virtual types of businesses, and as global competition heats up, the advantages continually move to those who know how to take the initiative in entirely new situations. These are people who can exert "entrepreneurial leadership". These next generation leaders will need this capability to take charge in rapidly changing dynamic environments. This is the same basic capability that is a hallmark of the politically savvy. Politically savvy entrepreneurs will know how to better cut across organizational, cultural and geographic lines to put together strategic alliances. Not only among individuals within the organization, but across multiple businesses as well.

The principles and concepts of the politically savvy should be quite useful to those who enter the business world with a strong entrepreneurial spirit. I hope they find this book valuable in their endeavors.

Lastly, the book will always be for those who care about making a difference in the world and want to make the most of their work lives.

Joel R. DeLuca, 1999

Preface to the First Edition

This book is fundamentally about leadership—but not the visible kind. Reading it will better equip you to be a force for change in your organization. It will provide you with the approaches and techniques to maximize your impact.

Good books abound which describe visible leadership. Bold decisions, symbolic actions, and charismatic presence are examples of what we'll call limelight* leadership. These traits refer to how leaders perform when the spotlight of attention is focused upon them. While leaders' visible actions are certainly important to organizational success, leadership is more than its limelight side.

Downward leadership is also well represented in today's press. That is, managers are portrayed as occupying formal positions responsible for several subordinates. Research evidence and advice are then provided to help managers carry out their official leadership roles. Again, while leaders' abilities to manage and motivate subordinates are critical to organizational success, leadership is also more than its downward side.

Leadership is actually multifaceted, and this book explores some of its less visible but equally vital sides. Although the methods addressed here also apply to traditional limelight leadership, they are primarily directed at what will be called "leadership behind-the-scenes." Such leadership, based on informal influence strategies, is the essence of political savvy.

*Before electricity, lime was heated to incandescence, which created a brilliant beam of light to illuminate actors on a stage.

Limelight leadership is public and includes formal meetings, official communications, and discussions. It is typically seen by a large number of employees and other stakeholders of the organization. On the flip side, only a few insiders possess the knowledge of the official leader's effectiveness behind-the-scenes in dealing with the sometimes harsh realities of organizational life. Delicate egos, vested interests, and protected turfs all require skilled attention. Political savvy refers to the unofficial influence approaches occurring out of sight in most organizations. Such influence goes beyond appearances and beyond subordinates toward other key individuals who shape decisions.

Political savvy is an essential leadership skill. Looking away from the glow of a company's few charismatic stars, like slipping behind a Broadway curtain, one can glimpse how much action in today's organizations occurs behind-the-scenes. It's accomplished by men and women at every level who want to make a difference and are willing to work around the bureaucracy and other barriers in their own organizations. Their skill typically goes unrecognized by the firm and, surprisingly, often by the individuals themselves!

The naturally Savvy frequently develop their skills unconsciously over their careers. For many of these individuals savvy skills are not worth investigating because, as in the words of one savvy executive, they're "just common sense." Since few people spend much time analyzing areas they consider common sense, the naturally Savvy's insight and behavior go unexamined. In truth, however, what is common sense for the intuitively Savvy is actually uncommon sense for the bulk of practicing managers.

One experienced leadership trainer, frustrated with natural leaders' inability to comprehend their own skills, wrote the following lament:

Preface

Lament against the Naturals

They are unaware
That their skills are rare
Thus, they do not turn
To help their fellows learn.
Claiming "it's common sense" is no defense
When others wallow in incompetence.
—Anonymous

Discussing political savvy is also difficult for another group—the very unsavvy, often believe politics is inherently immoral and thus they refuse to take part. The unsavvy don't see the extent to which informal influence is occurring behind-the-scenes. In fact they may actually cultivate a political blind spot. It's as if they need to believe that their organization and their own behaviors are highly rational and that technical merit alone suffices to sway decisions.

While this rational view is understandable in theory, there are risks associated with it in practice. A view that politics is negative leaves the political field to manipulators. Pretending "politics doesn't happen here" only tends to drive it underground, where it becomes even harder to manage.

Both groups, the unsavvy and the naturally Savvy, can end up placing barriers to the healthy functioning of the organization. The unsavvy don't participate. The naturally Savvy aren't systematic and don't develop the political skills of others.

Changing times cry out for individuals who are technically expert, managerially competent, and politically Savvy. Too many good ideas get chewed up by dysfunctional organization politics. Too many managerial improvements wither and die on the political vine, and too many talented individuals give up their innovative "spark" after several encounters with political predators. This book is written to give managers the means to improve their odds when fighting in their company's political jungles.

The subtitle mentions *systematic approaches*. This means the principles and techniques of the naturally Savvy are presented in a conscious, orderly, step-by-step fashion. In actuality, political savvy is "wild and woolly" and not rigid or structured. As practiced in organizations today, it's generally an art form. Art follows its own organic nature and resists being captured by mechanical rules. However, this book is based on the belief that every art form has an underlying discipline. By unraveling and attempting to make conscious the art of political savvy, individuals can create a useful foundation to build their own influence capacities.

The material comes from several sources. One is the author's twenty years of experience in both line and staff positions with a variety of public and private sector organizations. The book actually started with an investigation into the nature of strategic decision making across a broad set of organizations. The basic finding was labeled the Snowflake Theory of strategic decisions. It evolved from the fact that despite official policy manuals claiming otherwise, when the histories of various decisions were traced—like snowflakes— no two were exactly alike. The reasons given for this result were even more intriguing. Approximately 60 percent of the managers having insider knowledge said decisions were strongly influenced by what they called "political considerations" and approximately 90 percent said decisions were at least partially determined by organization politics.

This book also draws upon the growing body of scholarly research on power and politics in organizations. It is not designed to present an academic viewpoint, however. Substantial material comes from hundreds of candid interviews with individuals identified by colleagues as savvy and unsavvy. Additional material comes from political savvy workshops conducted over the last decade. The range of participants covered an organizational spectrum of big and small, public and private, but was limited to North American culture. Where possible, direct quotes from managers rather than research citations are used to elaborate key points.

Preface

This book is not for those who want quick tips on how to reach the top, nor is it for those interested in a deep abstract discussion of the subject. It's also not meant for individuals who want charisma or want to greatly increase their interpersonal skills. Contrary to popular opinion, charisma and interpersonal skills, while important, were not found to be central to becoming politically savvy. In fact, individuals with these qualities tend to rely on them too heavily, thereby hindering their development of savvy strategies. For those seeking such information, though, the Further Readings section contains several guides.

Instead, this book aims at pragmatic managers who seek better strategies to influence their organizations ethically and who want to develop this capability in others.

Managers, a term used throughout the text, refers to anyone who manages people, tasks, or projects. It, therefore, includes line and staff, executives and professionals. While the issues and techniques have wide applicability, the book is organized in a way that should be particularly useful to those in project management roles.

To explore how one effectively develops leadership behind the-scenes, two means are emphasized. First is the political savvy orientation without which all the strategy and tactics are useless. The essence of this orientation is to overcome viewing ethical politics as a paradox. To the surprise of some, engaging in politics doesn't mean being unethical. Savvy individuals are very active behind-the-scenes and have found a way to influence with integrity. They do not find it easy, but they do find it possible.

The second means is a practical set of tools. These tools are strategies, managerial techniques, and tactics used by the naturally Savvy but presented in a conscious, systematic fashion.

There are two ways for the reader to make a fast judgment of the potential usefulness of the book. Read chapter 12, the summary. If everything there sounds like common sense, then you may be intuitively savvy, and this book's value lies in making your skills more conscious and systematic. A stronger test is to jump immediately to the Chromium Project in chapter 4. Develop your solution and match it with that of the politically savvy individuals in chapter 5. If the results are the same, your natural savvy skills are probably solid, and this book would serve to capture what you do in ways that allow you to develop these skills in others.

The chapters are laid out in a natural progression from the political savvy orientation to basic strategies and then specific tactics. However, you can fruitfully enter most anywhere and work backwards or forwards. The book contains a lot of concepts, rather densely packed. Therefore, the material is probably best covered in several digestible increments, rather than one breeze-through reading. Major points are highlighted throughout the book by use of exhibits.

Unveiling all of what it means to succeed in organization politics is not possible in one book. Several volumes still wouldn't do the topic justice. While this book does not present the superhighway to political savvy stardom, it does try to cut a navigable path toward becoming more effective at leadership behind-the-scenes.

Joel DeLuca, 1992

Acknowledgments

This book has been in the making for over a decade, and I want to recognize some of the many people who contributed to its development. First and foremost, this book owes its existence to the hundreds of managers and professionals who candidly shared their experiences and views on organizational politics, change, and leadership.

The book got its spark from conversations with John Kimberly at Yale University. Richard Hackman, also then at Yale, through the fire of heated debate and through his passion for excellence, helped forge my thinking about organizational change.

Todd Jick at Harvard University and Andrew Kakabadse at the Crainfield School of Management in England have by their work on organizational politics encouraged my own. Stephen Stumpf at New York University has been a constant source of ideas and support throughout the development of the work. John Kotter's contributions at Harvard on the nature of leadership in today's organizations reinforced the directions I found myself heading in. The intellectual spirit behind this book is Kurt Lewin whose dictum "If you want to understand something, try to change it" has been a guiding force in my career.

I've had the privilege of working with a number of talented organizational change practitioners over the years whose practice helped shape my understanding of political savvy. Kathy Morris is a natural with the uncanny ability to grasp complex concepts and turn them into simple actions that change organizations. One of the best I've ever seen at political savvy in the trenches is Michael Kitson. Our years on the firing line co-strategizing corporate change in a Fortune top 20 corporation, have strengthened every aspect of this work.

In a similar vein, Stew Friedman has been a valuable contributor in testing these concepts in our work at evolving the leadership program in the Wharton School's MBA core curriculum at the University of Pennsylvania.

Several professionals made comments on earlier versions of the manuscript, in particular, Maria Arnone, Joseph DeLuca, George Morris, John Patriarca, and Joe Frigiola helped increase the usefulness and clarity of the ideas in the book. I also want to acknowledge colleagues Emmy Miller and Dudley Cooke who helped to refine several key ideas to make them more relevant to business executives.

Dawn Lowes graciously volunteered the arduous task of turning my hand written hieroglyphics into print. Sue Harner provided critical logistical support and Carol Ronnholm worked through countless revisions. I am indebted to them for their time, patience, and commitment to this project. Jacqulyne Hardiesty was essential in creating the second edition and deserves my sincerest gratitude for her calming patience and hard work.

PART ONE

Choosing to Become an Active, Ethical Player

> ...[L]eadership and power appear as two closely related concepts, and if we want to understand effective leadership, we may begin by studying the power motive in thought and action.
>
> —David C. McClelland, *Power: The Inner Experience*

Chapter 1

INTRODUCTION

Important changes that are shaping the nature of work in today's complex organizations demand that we become more sophisticated with respect to issues of leadership, power, and influence.

—John P. Kotter, *Power and Influence*

John Thompson slammed his beer mug on the table. "I just don't understand." He was sitting with his boss, Sam Reilly, in a local tavern after work.

"Take it easy, John, these things happen. There will be other projects."

"How can I take it easy?" said John. "We had everything going for us, the president said he wanted the Hydro Project, and we had strong management support. It would have given the company a real edge over our competition."

"I know," said Sam, "you and your staff worked very hard and did an excellent job on the technical analysis. You clearly showed the potential value of the project. But you know as well as I do that Larry Weesly in Marketing was beginning to see that it might have cut into his turf. When he said the project was too risky and then suggested a more conservative approach, the president had to pay attention. They go back a long way, and he has confidence in Larry's views."

"But Larry's proposal is built on thin air. I've looked at his numbers, and they're based on very shaky assumptions," responded John.

"You know that and I know that," said Sam, "but in the end its a judgment call, and we know whose judgment the president is going to side with."

John, still unconsoled, retorted, "Yes, but it's not right, it's not fair. Everybody loses. The shareholders lose, the company loses, the customers lose, and even the employees will eventually lose."

"Everybody but Larry," sighed Sam.

● ● ● ● ● ●

Kathy Kraften clinked her champagne glass with the others. "Congratulations, Kathy, to you and your staff," said her boss, Jake.

"I don't know how you did it, but you got the new Clarion Network Program approved and implemented on schedule. "

"Thank you, Jake," said Kathy, "but it's really no mystery. It seemed to be the right thing for the organization. My staff worked hard and we used common sense."

"I believe you, Kathy," responded Jake, "but the odds were against you from the beginning. You didn't have much backing from upper management. Even I was a bit doubtful. You also ran the risk of stepping on a lot of executive toes. Information that some of them used to have exclusive control over is now available to the whole organization."

The other team members chimed in with remarks such as "We knew that going in, but we really believed in what we were doing."

"I grant you that," said Jake, "but what really surprised me was how you got around Ann Vader. She was dead set against you and used every trick in the book to pull the plug on the pro-

Introduction

ject. She has a lot of influence, but she really ended up shooting herself in the foot the way she reacted at the last executive meeting."

"Well anyway," said Kathy, "the company now has a real chance to beat the competition. Employees can get information quicker, and customers can get faster responses. Hopefully, everybody wins."

"Everybody but Ann," smiled Jake.

••••••

These are two examples of actual events in the same organization. Almost every manager has had similar experiences sometime in his or her career. John Thompson and Kathy Kraften were both technically expert. Can the separate outcomes be accounted for by luck? Yes, to the extent that organizations are complex. There are many forces, both visible and non-visible, that affect decisions; therefore, luck is always a factor. The real question is whether certain actions taken by John and Kathy affected the odds of their success. The answer from the perspective of this book is a clear and definite yes!

Political Savvy as a Key Dimension of Leadership

Leadership is a hot topic in management circles. So far, attention has focused on the more visible roles leaders play when they're in the organization limelight. Limelight leadership includes having an inspiring vision of the company's future, managing culture by symbolic actions, generating commitment by practicing Management By Walking Around (MBWA), and building management teams through open communication and participative methods. The list grows daily.

Each behavior mentioned above is important to leadership. Yet, some managers do all the right things in their visible roles and still have little organizational impact. Then there are low profile managers who often violate principles of limelight leadership yet make a tremendous impact on the organization. The press is understandably enamored of highly visible leaders who turn their companies around. Attention to these dramatic exploits, however, can skew opinion as to what really makes the day-in, day-out difference in organizations.

In actuality, the success of high performing companies results as much from what happens behind-the-scenes as from leaders' more visible actions. The difference between John Thompson and Kathy Kraften is this behind-the-scenes dimension of leadership-*political savvy.*

Chapter 2

UNDERSTANDING YOUR OWN POLITICAL STYLE

All classifications made by man are arbitrary, artificial, and false. But an equally simple consideration shows that these classifications are useful and indispensable; and above all, that they are unavoidable because they correspond to an innate tendency in our way of thinking.

—Egon Friedel

Stepping-stones make it possible to cross turbulent political waters. Observers who don't know that the stones lie just below the surface may think one is walking on water. The consciously Savvy know better. Before individuals can strengthen their own political savvy, awareness of their political style and that of others is essential. This chapter addresses one of the most intriguing aspects of organization politics: most managers appear to be unaware that they even have a political style! If they are aware, seldom has conscious choice entered into that style.

Popular Beliefs about Organization Politics

In political savvy workshops, managers are asked for their gut reactions to the phrase organization politics (see exhibit 1).

Popular Beliefs about Organization Politics

Popular Beliefs about Organization Politics	
• Manipulation	• Petty Personal Squabbles
• "I'll scratch your back if you scratch mine"	• Looking Good without Substance
• Looking Out for # 1	• Back-Room Decisions
• Destructiveness	• Power Plays
• The Organization's Soap Opera	• Natural Human Behavior
• Covert Under-the-Table Deals	• Behind-the-Scenes Maneuvering
• Backstabbing	• Brownnosing
• One-Upmanship	• Clever Operators
• Deceitfulness	• Influence Attempts
• Turf Battles	• Hidden Agendas

exhibit 1

All in all, their responses do not paint a pretty picture. Major themes revolve around back-room dealings and personal gain at the expense of others and the organization. It's no wonder so many managers avoid organization politics. Some try to ignore it, many try to stay out of it, and most wish it would just go away. However, as one CEO of an oil company put it, "As long as organizations have people in them, there will be politics."

Curiously, when asked if they want to engage in organization politics, the overwhelming majority responded with an emphatic NO! Yet when asked if they would like to become more politically savvy, a similarly overwhelming majority responded with a definite YES!

So it seems that individuals want to avoid the negatives of organization politics and gain the positives of political savvy. To do so it is necessary first to understand the diverse political styles found in organizations.

Managers often know their leadership style in terms of autocratic Theory X versus collaborative Theory Y, yet ask them about their political style and they will respond with a blank stare. Further discussion reveals that most have seldom thought through how they manage from an organization politics perspective.

After encouraging managers across a wide range of organizations to describe their behavior and after observing them in action, one sees certain patterns related to political styles begin to emerge. Two basic factors, which account for much of the variety in styles, stand out. The first refers to the action orientation toward organization politics. The second centers on the person's value orientation toward political behavior. Hundreds of organizational interviews and experiences show that these two factors are frequently related.

Action Orientation

Many individuals are not very active when it comes to organization politics. They respond to events as they occur but generally keep their heads down and avoid getting involved. Others sit back with their eyes open to the political scene and try to predict what might happen so they can be prepared ahead of time. A few go much further and initiate strong action in the political arena. Although the actual degree of activity varies from situation to situation, people often express clear preferences in terms of how active they want to become.

Value Orientation

The basic feeling many executives express toward organization politics is distaste. "Why can't I just do my job and keep the politics out of it," remarked one prominent plant manager. Others seem to accept it as a natural fact of organizational life. "It's unfortunate, but whenever you put two humans together, there's bound to be some type of one-upmanship going on. That's politics," commented a middle manager in a marketing department. Still others actually enjoy the liveliness associated with organization politics. "I find it exciting, it's where the action is, and it's the only way I've seen anything significant ever get done," said the CEO of a pharmaceutical company. Thus the value orientation varies from *negative* to *neutral* to *positive*.

Action and Value Interrelationships

Different values combine with different levels of activeness to produce a diversity of political styles. It's easy to see how people's values about organization politics are likely to shape the political style they adopt. The more negatively managers view politics, the less likely they are to engage in it. The reverse is not true. It turns out that the activeness of a person is not a good predictor of how he or she values organization politics.

THE POLITICAL STYLE GRID

Combining the three value and three action orientations leads to the Political Style Grid (see exhibit 2). The vertical dimension indicates the action orientation in increasing order from responds to predicts to initiates.

The horizontal dimension designates the value orientation and moves from negative to neutral to positive. This configuration results in the nine basic styles shown on the Grid. Let's begin at the bottom.

Understanding Your Own Political Style

The Political Style Grid

Politics viewed as:

Action Orientation		Negative	Neutral	Positive
		Machiavellian	**Responsible**	**Leader**
	Initiates	- Manipulator - Looks out for #1	- Obligation - Comes with Territory	- Play Maker - Impact Player
		Protector	**Speculator**	**Advisor**
	Predicts	- File Builder - Defensive	- Grapeviner	- Counselor
		Cynic	**Fatalist**	**Spectator**
	Responds	- I told you so - Gossip	- Que Sera Sera	- Fan - Encourager

exhibit 2

Cynic

The cynic style often results when one sees too many projects go to slick presenters and too many promotions go to yesmen. As a manager in a research and development (R&D) department put it, "To be successful around here, all you have to do is look good in project reviews and tell the boss what he wants to hear."

The Cynic wants no part of organization politics and, therefore, is low on the action dimension. The Cynic typically views organization politics as a win-lose proposition and values it negatively. Individuals with a strong cynic orientation frequently believe they are just being realistic: "Look, I'm tired of beating my head against the wall. It just doesn't pay and I've got better things to do with my time," observed a professional actuary in an insurance firm.

The longer one has been in the typical organization and the more battles one has lost, the more likely one is to develop a cynical style. Nothing is inherently wrong with this style, since it is often warranted by the manager's personal experience. When Cynics predominate in an organization, however, vitality drains out. People with this style seldom go the extra mile except under duress, and even then, they tend to avoid taking risks because, as one manager in an art museum put it, "There is little to gain if you succeed and a lot to lose if you fail." Unfortunately for organizations populated with this style, most of the available creativity channels into activities off the job. Talented managers with a cynic style often have elaborate hobbies outside the office and view work merely as a way of earning a paycheck. When an initiative goes wrong, they often respond with the motto of the cynical style, "I told you so."

Fatalist

Next, moving across the Political Style Grid, is the Fatalist. This style is like the Cynic's in that the manager initiates little action, but it differs in not viewing politics as inherently negative. "Look, I know these kinds of things go on; you just have to roll with the punches," is the way one manager put it after his less qualified peer was promoted over him. The Fatalist assumes politics is a fact of life. John Thompson's boss in the opening vignette of this book illustrated this style well when he said, "These things happen. There will be other projects." At its best, the fatalist style allows individuals to endure in the face of negative politics. Managers with this style can last a long time in the organization and seldom succumb to the burnout that plagues the Cynic. As one executive in a staff position said, "Hey, I don't let it get to me, life's too short, and there's not much you can do about it."

While the fatalist political style fosters endurance, it tends not to foster action in the political arena. Fatalists seldom do anything about the political dynamics of the organization. "Why bother when the odds are stacked against you? Just do your job and hope for the best." The Fatalist assumes little can be done to affect politics and approaches it with stoic acceptance. Many professionals and technically oriented managers drift toward the fatalist style.

Spectator

Spectators like to watch but don't like to play. These managers view the organization as a vast human soap opera and root for their favorite characters. "Politics in this department is fascinating. You should see what Larry is trying to do to Mary, but I think Mary can outmaneuver him," remarked one professional in a legal function. Spectators frequently have enough political savvy to appreciate a good move. From the same professional: "You should have seen the way Mary finessed Larry at the Management Committee meeting last Thursday. Larry had gotten together this impressive bunch of data showing why Mary's financial billing project couldn't work, but Mary was ready for him. She played her ace in the hole and showed how two of the company's competitors were already using the new analytical procedure successfully. She came out way on top."

The Spectator assumes politics can be positive but generally avoids risks. Spectators provide emotional support and consolation to those taking a more active role. They are typically the first to suggest going out for a drink after a political loss or to pat someone on the back after a political win.

Protector

Moving up to the middle level of the Grid, we come to the protector style. The Protector views politics negatively, as the Cynic does, but takes a more active approach. Rather than giving up and awaiting the worst, the Protector does something about it. "I've already been burned twice, and I'm not going to let it happen again," remarked a government administrator.

Protectors have their fingers in the wind and actively try to predict the political weather and defend themselves against it. A signpost of Protectors is that they frequently have more file cabinets or saved e-mails than anybody else. In speaking about such an individual in an advertising firm an executive said, "After the Glassex account fiasco Jim began to document everything. He writes memo after memo to prove what his involvement was and wasn't. The next time something goes wrong, he wants to be able to demonstrate without a doubt that it wasn't his fault."

One advantage of this style is that in a chaotic situation Protectors generally have the best records of what actually happened. The downside is it can lead to bureaucracy and even the yes-man syndrome. Managers who assume politics is inherently negative and don't want to be hurt by it can build in too many checks and double checks. They use up valuable time burying the system in paperwork and excessive numbers of approvals.

Protectors are often "fence sitters" in regard to new ideas. They read the political cues first and then go with whichever side seems to be in political favor. The hallmark of the extreme Protector is the ready yes sir to the boss's suggestions.

Speculator

The Speculator is also active in predicting organization politics. This manager is less concerned with self-protection, however, and more interested in the political dynamics themselves. As a steel company executive remarked, "Sure there's a lot of politics around here; that's what makes the place interesting. I stay out of it for the most part, but I do enjoy handicapping the players, you know, predicting who's trying to do what to whom and all that." The pure Speculator almost treats organization politics as a game show, trying to guess the answers and predict the winners.

Speculators are frequently sources of the organizational grapevine. Speculators like foretelling who is likely to get the vacant position and which project will receive budget approval. On the upside, the Speculator keeps informal communications going and finds zest in organizational life that may be lacking in the job itself. On the downside, this style manager creates rumors and distracts the organization from its task. Speculators are particularly active during restructurings. A manager in a wholesale clothing firm actually boasted, "I predicted the last three CEOs and started a rumor that may have helped one person being seen as best for the job." While most Speculators don't go to such extremes, they do tend to assume politics is a fact of organizational life, so why not talk about it.

Advisor

While the Speculator is a bit of a voyeur, the Advisor operates by providing managers with suggestions that are politically astute. Advisors use their interest in predicting as a way to influence others' actions. "Hey, listen, I want this place to be successful, and if I can help those people trying to make it work, then that's what I'll do" is the way one rising manager in a fast-food corporation put it.

Advisors can be interested third parties or subordinates,

but, more frequently, they are peers or senior executives. As one vice president in a financial services firm remarked, "We have a lot of talented young managers who don't know the first thing about how to make change really happen around here. As an old war horse, I want to help them get their innovations brought into the system." Advisors typically stay off center stage and prefer to work by counseling others.

Advisors generally assume politics is not inherently negative or even a sad fact of life. Instead, they try to find the win-win alternative for the key players and the company. They believe organizations are much more than technical and rational systems. "One thing you have to remember is that organizations are created by people and run by people-people, not machines or money. As long as they are made up of people, managing the politics of human nature is how things actually get done," commented a senior executive in a shipping business.

At their best, Advisors guide others through the political mazes. At their worst, they avoid taking responsibility for actions or for decisions that shape the organization's destiny.

Machiavellian

Across the Grid's top layer are the highly active players. One group works in the Machiavellian style. Most people imagine this style when they think of organization politics. *Webster's Dictionary* defines *Machiavellian* with words such as *deceitful*, and *unscrupulous*, *cunning* or *guile*. Actually, in writing about politics, the sixteenth-century Italian statesman Niccolo Machiavelli was rather neutral. His classic treatise on the subject was called *The Prince*. But, over the centuries, his principles have become associated with ambitious manipulators. So even though poor Niccolo didn't intend it, the negative connotation of being Machiavellian fits modern-day usage.

What distinguishes this and the remaining two styles from the six previous ones is that these managers take the initiative. They don't just watch or predict; instead, they jump into organization politics with both feet.

Understanding Your Own Political Style

An individual with an extreme Machiavellian style, or Mach for short, assumes that organizational life is a win-lose proposition. As one fast-track manager in the entertainment industry put it, "It's a dog-eat-dog world in this company. They hired a bunch of ambitious talent, and we all know the pyramid gets narrow at the top. Since someone has to win, it might as well be me." Those with the Mach style are the Darth Vaders in the organization whom people fear. It's this style that has given politics a label so sinister that it obscures the positive side of organization politics.

Organizations may unintentionally create Mach managers. One president of a large consulting firm summarized his promotion system as, "We try to get top talent in here, pit them against each other in the great tradition of the American competitive spirit, and let the cream rise to the top." Unfortunately, such simplistic approaches often breed competitors and "turf builders" rather than team builders. "Why should I help Jerry? He's likely to get the credit and move up faster than me," explained a young professional in the same consulting firm.

All too often, the interests of the organization get lost as Machs concentrate on advancing their own personal goals. Shifts away from the interests of the organization toward personal winning lead to the nightmare about Machs: They will go to any length to advance over others. An executive in a construction firm told of an incident where "Hank deliberately held back on supplying Jan the steel beams just so she would miss her contract deadline and look bad to the president. Oh, he had all the right excuses to look innocent, but it was clear to several of us what was really going on. Missing that deadline cost the company thousands but Hank came out smelling like a rose." The Mach style is very active and, if too prevalent, can greatly damage the organization. One department head in a cosmetic firm observed, "There is so much back-biting, brownnosing, and gamesmanship going on around here I'm not sure anyone gives a damn about the customer anymore."

Responsible

A person with a responsible style is also very active in the political arena, although often reluctantly. Responsibles feel a strong obligation to do what is best for the organization. They view organizations as fundamentally human rather than rational systems and, therefore, aren't surprised by the existence of politics. "It comes with the territory of being an executive," said one hospital administrator, typifying the attitude of the responsible style. There are many successful managers with this style since they are generally savvy about the various political maneuvers occurring and how to deal with them.

The responsible style often arises in reaction to the Mach style. "I dislike politics as much as the next guy and would prefer to stay out of it, but I'll be damned if I'm going to let good ideas go down the tubes because of some overly ambitious S.O.B."

The Responsibles are like the white blood cells in the system, protecting it as much as they can from the cancerous Machs. The underlying credo of the true Responsible is the saying "all it takes for evil to conquer is for good men to stand by and do nothing." Those with a responsible style feel an obligation to ensure that the interests of the organization are paramount in key decisions. This represents the upside of the Responsible style. When successful, Responsibles give the organization a sense of integrity and ethics, that generates organizational loyalty among ever-watchful employees. The downside is that Responsibles frequently act from feelings of obligation rather than desire. This style can therefore result in a constant sense of weariness and, eventually, to premature executive burnout.

Leader

Labeling this style *leader* is deliberate. It dramatizes a key point of this book: While some leaders may seem to be above

Understanding Your Own Political Style

politics, there is generally a high correlation between how others rank a person's leadership and how they rank that person's political savvy. The two often go hand in hand. Of the active styles, the Leader is the most positive one when it comes to valuing organization politics.

This style can exist at any level in the organization. Like the Responsibles, Leaders tend to assume that organizations are primarily people systems rather than technical ones. They believe strongly that progress depends on aligning the personal interests of individuals with each other (team building) and with the interests of the organization (commitment generation).

Although well aware of the negative side of organization politics, the Leader views people as basically good and wanting to contribute to the success of the organization. As a CEO of a large computer firm put it, "I believe most people desire to make a difference. Sure we have the overly ambitious types, but who doesn't? My job is to see that their drive is channeled for the good of the company."

In management circles, there is a saying that the difference between leadership and management is that "you manage things and lead people." Individuals with the Leader style seem to understand this difference implicitly. The Leader style coincides with one historian's view of the Founding Fathers who wrote the United States Constitution:

> *They were a unique body of men who were neither illusioned or disillusioned about human nature. They designed a template to bring out the best of the nation's citizens such as autonomy, freedom, diversity, and a sense of industry and enterprise. At the same time they built in checks and balances necessary to keep citizens' baser instincts at bay.*[1]

The Leader strongly believes in searching for the win-win solutions in which everyone gains something. While those having negative or neutral views on politics often begin by looking for the middle ground, Leaders start with creativity, not compromise. They don't acquiesce; they act. Leaders are the playmakers in the organization. By creating innovative ways to combine and satisfy apparently opposed interests, they break logjams and make things happen that wouldn't normally occur. Those who use the Leader political style do compromise but as the court of last resort.

Those with the Leader style can be highly visible and have limelight qualities, but more often they are low-key and work steadily and quietly behind-the-scenes. As one executive commented about an automotive CEO, "Ed is not charismatic or even a good speaker, and he keeps a low profile. All he does is get things done. I don't know how he did it, but he's made more productive change around here than the last two flashy CEOs put together."

There is a myth that to be a Leader one has to have a magnetic personality and be at the top of the hierarchy. While this type of leader gets the lion's share of attention, there is more practical truth to the notion that effective Leaders exist at all levels in the organization. The common thread among them has more to do with political savvy than charisma. The other common thread among Leaders is that they actively care about something larger than themselves. Machs, on the other hand are seldom able to rise above their own narrow and ambitious self interest.

Limitations of the Political Style Grid

Identifying one's normal style is an important prerequisite to becoming more politically savvy. Yet, as the quote at the beginning of the chapter states, categories are useful but artificial. Their usefulness comes from being taken as guides and not as reality. Otherwise, the squares of the Grid end up boxing people into rigid stereotypes, instead of supporting the notion of flexible political styles.

In real life, managers can display all nine styles. An executive who normally had a responsible style gave an example of a situation that called for protective style behavior:

Understanding Your Own Political Style

Business was bad; cutbacks were coming, and executives were scrambling to survive. The important thing became not being associated with unsuccessful projects. Blame was in the air, and I had to learn how to duck. I documented absolutely everything I did. The "cc" list[2] became my ally. Other executives knew exactly what I was involved in. It worked for awhile, but the rug was pulled out from under me. Profits dropped further in my division due to the supplier strike that I warned the company about. See, I even wrote this memo predicting a strike and recommending alternate suppliers be developed. The company didn't act, and the strike occurred, leaving us short of critical raw materials. Still, they needed a scapegoat for the upcoming board meeting, and I was history.

How Different Styles View Each Other

Individuals who are unaware tend to assume their normal style is the only realistic one. As a result, they view other styles in biased ways. Those with a Responsible style, for example, can view Spectators with distaste as voyeurs who enjoy the soap opera but do little about it. Advisors can see Protectors as organization deadwood who dam up the work flow with a tangled defensive bureaucracy. When encountering any of the active styles, Fatalists often snicker and wonder what all the fuss is about. Machiavellians generally view those with a Leader style as naive Pollyannas. Thus, political style is not an arena in which opposites attract. It's more one in which political styles of a feather flock together.

Cynics distrust even those with a Leader style, for in practice the public behavior of the Machiavellian frequently imitates that of the Leader. The Cynic, assuming that politics is inherently self-serving, may view Leaders as Machs in disguise. Therefore, when a Leader reports to a strong Cynic, trouble brews. One Cynic manager had a subordinate with a Leader style who successfully resolved a difficult interdepartmental conflict. The subordinate unblocked a costly stalemate by dealing directly with the manager in the other department, thus bypassing the normal chain of command. His Cynic manager remarked, "Sure, John got the problem solved, but he also got some glory and undermined my authority. I don't know what he's up to, but from now on I'm keeping a tighter leash on him." The result was bewilderment and frustration for the subordinate. It takes considerable political savvy skill to maintain a Leader style in such a situation.

Political Styles and Political Savvy

Long-established firms are more likely to be populated with Protectors, Speculators, Cynics, and Fatalists. That is, a large segment of the managerial population views politics as negative or, at best, neutral, and limits its involvement to predicting. Managers with these predominant styles are rarely seen as politically savvy by others. An executive commenting on one such individual said, "I'm not sure what happened to Ted. He was technically brilliant, but he couldn't influence the organization to get his ideas accepted. It's a shame; he had a lot of potential."

Individuals regarded as politically savvy generally have orientations in the responsible-leader-advisor areas. "Jim is not the smartest manager we have or even the best interpersonally, but he seems to have the know-how to get his projects through the system better than others" is a typical comment regarding managers with these styles. They tend to be more active and more positive toward organization politics.

Pike Fish and Conscious Choice of Style

An excursion into another field summarizes the basic point of this chapter.

In the early 1950s, there were a series of experiments by psychologists attempting to understand behavioral flexibility. They used a species of fish known as pike in their studies. First, a pike was put in a large tank of water. Now it so happens that pike love guppies, as sort of their equivalent to potato chips.

Understanding Your Own Political Style

When guppies were put in the tank, the pike immediately charged and gobbled them up. The psychologists, being a bit like pranksters, then placed a clear glass pane (invisible to the pike) in the middle of the tank. With the pike at one end they dumped guppies into the other end and watched. Well, when the pike saw the guppies, it went straight for them, accelerating to full speed, and then—WHAM!—it crashed into the invisible glass wall. Dazed for only a moment, it again took off for the guppies—again WHAM! into the glass wall. Since pike aren't overloaded with complex neural connections, it repeated this over and over. Slowly, however, it began to learn. The pike determined from its own experience, literally from the "school of hard knocks," that it couldn't get the guppies.

The psychologists weren't quite finished yet. Next, they removed the pane of glass. The guppies were now just a quick lunge away. However, something unexpected happened. The pike didn't go after the guppies, not even those swimming near its jaws! The pike had learned too well from past experience that it couldn't get the guppies. It learned so well in fact, that it became an assumption below its awareness. In some of the experiments, the pike actually starved to death!

The point of this fish story is that we humans also learn from our experiences. Political style is generally developed from a set of experiences early in a person's career. Many individuals have knocked their heads against organization walls and made assumptions about organization politics. These assumptions have gone so deep that they have become unconscious political styles. When was the last time you were in a conversation about the topic of political style?

The Political Style Grid is one device to help surface any "pike fish assumptions" about politics. Dealings with managers who have high potential demonstrate time and time again that two crucial steps must be taken before specific political strategies and tactics can be frankly discussed. First, underlying assumptions about organization politics need to be examined. Second, conscious choices about the appropriate political style for a given situation need to be made. Some managers routinely take these steps. For others, however, this awareness raising is not as easy as it sounds. Obstacles to political awareness are the rule more than the exception, and they frequently lead to a self-deceptive political blind spot. Holding to the negative stereotype and not realizing that politics can also be positive fosters this blind spot. It can work in such subtle ways that people ignore the informal influence attempts going on all around them, and they can even miss how they themselves participate in such attempts much of the time. Their typical response is: There's no politics around here.

The political blind spot is tricky. It fosters denial. It is such an inhibiting factor in developing political savvy skills that it is the major focus of the next chapter.

CHAPTER NOTES

[1] William Peters, A More Perfect Union: The Making of the United States Constitution (New York: Crown Publishers, 1987), 24.

[2] The list of names at the bottom of a memo referring to whom copies were sent.

Chapter 3

THE POLITICAL BLIND SPOT

Power tends to corrupt and absolute power corrupts absolutely.

—Lord Acton, *Letter to Bishop Creighton*

Weakness tends to corrupt, and impotence corrupts absolutely.

—Edgar Friedenberg, *Coming of Age in America*

John Thompson's frustration in the opening lines of chapter one indicates the presence of the political blind spot. Interestingly, despite Kathy Kraften's success with the Clarion Network Program, her view that it was "common sense" may also indicate that she has the political blind spot as defined in exhibit 3.

> **The Political Blind Spot**
>
> Not consciously seeing the extent to which informal influence shapes the decision making process

exhibit 3

Political Savvy

The first step in increasing political savvy is to understand the predominant political style one has developed over the years. The next step is to overcome the major blocks to adopting a political savvy orientation. This chapter addresses two mental blocks that show up repeatedly in workshops for high-potential managers. Taken together, these mental blocks prevent many individuals from wanting to see or acknowledge the political aspect of organizational life.

The Moral Block

The chief reason cited by managers for not actively engaging in organization politics is that they find it morally reprehensible. Lord Acton's quote at the beginning of this chapter captures the major concern. In this same vein, a glass manufacturing manager summed up his feelings as, "I'm here to do my job; organization politics is destructive, and I want to feel good when I see myself in the mirror each morning, so leave me out."

In seminars dealing with organization politics, managers are asked a series of questions. One example is How many of you believe you have high needs for achievement? Almost every hand quickly goes up. Next, they are asked How many of you want to feel the camaraderie associated with being a part of a high-performing team? Again, most hands are raised. Then they are asked, How many of you want power in the organization? Half of the time not a single hand is raised and people glance awkwardly at each other. The other half of the time one or two hands go up tentatively, most often prefaced by questions of interpretation or lengthy explanations.

Do these responses indicate that managers don't really want power? Hardly: extensive studies by researchers such as David McClelland[1] demonstrate significant power needs as well as achievement and affiliation (team membership) needs among the majority of managers. The low response in public-settings is just another indication of the distaste associated with organization politics. One manager sent an excerpt from George Orwell's 1984 (see exhibit 4) as her view of those who want power. While extreme, this view lurks in the minds of many and will be referred to in other chapters.

A Perspective on Power

Chapter One
IGNORANCE IS STRENGTH

Throughout recorded time, and probably since the end of the Neolithic Age, there have been three kinds of people in the world, the High, the Middle, and the Low.

The aims of these three groups are entirely irreconcilable. The aim of the High is to remain where they are. The aim of the Low is to abolish all distinctions and create a society in which all men shall be equal. They (the High) are then overthrown by the Middle, who enlist the Low on their side by pretending to them that they are fighting for Liberty and Justice. As soon as they reached their objective, the Middle thrust the Low back into their old position of servitude, and themselves become the High.

'Now tell me why we cling to power. What is our motive? Why should we want power? Go on, speak," he added as Winston remained silent.

"You are ruling over us for our own good," he said feebly. "You believe that human beings are not fit to govern themselves, and therefore—"

He started and almost cried out. A pang of pain had shot through his body. O'Brien had pushed the lever of the dial up to thirty-five.

"That was stupid, Winston, stupid!, he said. "You should know better than to say a thing like that."

"Now I will tell you the answer to the question. It is this. The Party seeks power entirely for its own sake. We are not interested in the good of others; we are interested solely in power. Not wealth or luxury or long life or happiness; only power, pure

> power. The German Nazis and the Russian Communists came very close to us in their methods, but they never had the courage to recognize their own motives. Power is not a means; it is an end. The object of persecution is persecution. The object of torture is torture. The object of power is power. Now do you begin to understand me?"
>
> *George Orwell, 1984*

exhibit 4

The desire for power is too often associated with excessive ambition and manipulation. Some individuals believe that there is nothing inherently wrong with manipulation. As one department head said, "Everybody manipulates; that's how things get done. Any time you change something you manipulate." This view has some merit as most dictionaries first define manipulation in neutral terms. However, secondary definitions include phrases such as unfair tactics, deceitful procedures, and undue influence.

The negative connotation of the term manipulation lies at the heart of the moral block. A substantial number of managers assume that being active in organization politics means being a manipulator. Out of a sense of personal integrity they refuse to take part. Managers with a moral block seldom become involved enough to develop their savvy skills. Those regarded as politically savvy, however, take a different view. As one savvy executive exclaimed, "I want to impact the hell out of this place. It's my job, but I don't want to manipulate."

Manipulation versus Influence

When managers are asked if they want to manipulate the organization' most say no. When they are asked if they want to influence the organization, most say yes. To slice through this Gordian[2] knot of confusion, one must make a pragmatic distinction between manipulation and influence. When politically reluctant managers are able to do this, it often cracks the moral block.

Influence can be portrayed as a continuum as it is in exhibit 5. There, manipulation is shown to be a part of, but not the major segment of, the continuum. *Savvy individuals don't inherently equate influence with manipulation.* While heeding the alarm sounded in Lord Acton's quote about power, they don't want to fall into the opposite trap indicated by Edgar Friedenberg's quote about weakness. As an executive in an aerospace corporation remarked, "Of course I try to influence this organization, that's what I'm here for, but I see no reason to resort to manipulation." Managers who don't understand the difference implied in this remark typically don't see influence as a continuum. The inability to differentiate types of influence is exactly what keeps so many people from becoming active in the political arena. As a result, their ability to become skilled at leadership behind-the-scenes is greatly diminished.

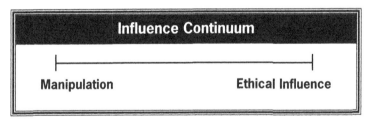

exhibit 5

Manipulation is only one form of influence. How does a manager tell the difference between influence and manipulation? Well, there has been a great deal of argument on the topic, however, the gist of the difference may be summed up in an imperfect but simple rule of thumb shown by the question in exhibit 6.

Political Savvy

Manipulation vs Ethical Influence
Rule of Thumb **If they knew what you were planning, would they let you?**

exhibit 6

If the answer to this question is no, then probably some type of manipulation is being used. If the answer is yes, then ethical influence is more likely to be at work. Ethical influence occurs when others know what you are trying to influence them toward and why. Politically savvy managers operate primarily in the ethical end of the influence continuum. Does this mean they never engage in manipulation? No, because the organizational world is too complex to be seen in simple black and white terms. They often struggle with moral dilemmas before taking action. One way to view the moral grayness of the real world is illustrated in exhibit 7.

Ethical Situations		
Means	**Ends**	**Outcomes**
Ethical	Ethical	⟶ Savvy
Unethical	Ethical	⟶ Moral Crisis
Unethical	Unethical	⟶ Machiavellian

exhibit 7

From this perspective, moral and ethical issues can be examined in terms of conflicts between means and ends. If the ends and means are both ethical then there is no moral crisis. Most politically savvy behavior can fit in this category and will be the major focus of the remaining chapters. Managers who have strong negative assumptions about organization politics seldom believe this category is truly possible. Therefore, they avoid trying to influence the organization beyond what is allowed by a strict and narrow interpretation of their formal job description.

Next comes the vexing category labeled "ethical ends but manipulative means". This is the ends-justify-the-means category so infamously occupied by those professing situational ethics. Since the manipulating Machiavellians frequently use this phrase to justify their actions, managers generally shy away from this category. Yet, politically astute people struggle with these situations. "I didn't want to tell Jack in front of all his people that his department was likely to be phased out in two years. We are not entirely sure yet and it would just demoralize them. When the question came up, I sidestepped it and just told them to keep up the good work," said one manager confronted in a public forum. This manager felt guilty about what he said, but he believed it was the best response until he could talk with Jack in private.

When we tell our kids that Santa Claus and the tooth fairy are real, we are acting as though the ends justify the means. Each time we tell our spouses we like a present when we don't or tell our hosts that a tasteless dish is delicious, we are also in this category. Rather than avoid this dilemma in organizational life, savvy individuals take it head on. They deal with feelings of guilt, question their own motivations and struggle with determining what's best for the organization. The quote in exhibit 8 comes from a person who faced many such situations. The Savvy use the spirit of Lincoln's quote to fine-tune and strengthen their own moral development.

> ***You don't learn to deal with ethical dilemmas by avoiding them.***
> — Abraham Lincoln

exhibit 8

They refuse to believe in a black and white organizational world, and they learn how to operate in the gray zones.

Savvy individuals do, however, draw the line and take a stand against the third category. When both the means and ends are unethical, there is no moral dilemma. The person or group is out for their own interests and will use any means to attain their agendas. This is the high-Mach zone. The skilled Machs, however, are clever at disguising their true motives in terms of both means and ends. They use ethical words and appearances merely as tools to achieve their goals. As a young manager in a federal agency commented on a rising star in the organization: "Alex is one of the most charming people you'd ever want to meet, but I learned about his true colors the hard way. Once, I constructively challenged a proposed direction he wanted to take for a key project. Most of top management agreed with me and Alex was very reassuring, but a week later Alex had me transferred to a new assignment for 'development purposes.' Last I heard, the project was back to Alex's original direction."

In sum, the Savvy avoid the third category and search for numerous ways to stay in the first one. When they do find themselves facing circumstances in the second category where they question whether the ends justify the means, they struggle. Often they will talk to mentors or trusted peers. Their decision is generally based upon their conscious judgment of what's best for the overall situation. Savvy managers take personal responsibility for this type of judgment call.

The Rational Block

The chief argument of those managers with the rational block is "I shouldn't have to do anything more than my job description. The technical merits of my work should be enough." Who can blame them for this type of thinking? After all, aren't organizations designed to be logical and task based? If so, it's only common sense that the arguments with the best logical and technical merits should win out. This is a particularly strong belief in engineering, manufacturing, and research and development organizations. As one young engineer in a computer business said, "I work hard and present the facts as I see them; then, it's for those higher up to make the decision. That's the only way the system can work."

Exhibit 9 is an excerpt from an interview in *Time* magazine with Sir Brian Urquart. He was awarded the 1988 Nobel Peace Prize for his diplomatic efforts around the world's hot spots in the Middle East, Afghanistan, and Cyprus, among others. He was being asked about early career experiences that shaped his own sense of political savvy.

Excerpt from an Interview with Sir Brian Urquart

Q. Perhaps it's not too widely known that you were the young intelligence officer portrayed in Cornelious Ryan's A Bridge Too Far. What led you to advise against the ill-fated British attack on Arnhem, in German-occupied Holland?

A. I had come to the conclusion that at all levels the attack would be totally disastrous. It didn't take a great deal of brains to see that. Airborne troops were going to land 60 miles ahead of the ground troops and take three main bridges over three big rivers, Then the relieving ground troops had to go across low country, We learned that two of the best Panzer divisions in the German army, the 9th and 10th S.S. Panzer Divisions, were refitting right where the 1st Airborne Division was going to land. I couldn't see the strategic point of that operation.

Q. Did Field Marshal Montgomery get the advice?

A. He got it from a lot of people. I merely advised my own general, General Browning, who was in charge of the whole Market Garden operation. I said, "Look here, you've got to rethink this. It's going to be a mess." That was completely overruled. Montgomery wanted to have a British masterstroke to end the war. When you're young, you believe that a good argument will win the day, and of course it doesn't. It was a terrible experience because an immense number of soldiers were killed, 12,000 as I remember. I was greatly disillusioned because I then realized that people in high positions were not necessarily always motivated by wisdom and concern for the common cause, but in fact could be motivated by other less desirable emotions, like vanity, ambition and a desire to score a point off somebody.

exhibit 9

The key line relevant to the current discussion is "When you're young, you believe that a good argument will win the day, and of course it doesn't." What is "of course" to this Nobel Prize winner is, unfortunately, not that obvious to managers with the rational block. In fact, for many such managers the rational assumption that a good argument based upon facts and logic should carry the day is so deeply ingrained that it has become a "pike fish assumption" and is not even questioned, much less felt as a block.

When interviews with those identified as politically savvy are compared with those considered unsavvy, a basic difference in perspective appears. Each views the fundamental definition of an organization in a subtly, but powerfully different way (see exhibit 10).

Two Views of Organizations

I. Organizations are *rational* systems that use humans in them.

II. Organizations are *human* systems attempting to act in a rational way.

---

exhibit 10

When unsavvy managers with strong beliefs in rational thought are presented with the first definition, their general

The Political Blind Spot

response is, "Of course, how could it be otherwise?" When savvy individuals are presented with the second definition, their general response is, "Of course, how could it be otherwise?" When a mixed group of savvy and unsavvy managers is presented with both definitions, heated discussions often take place. Some managers try to say the differences between the two definitions are merely semantics. They become frustrated and call to get off the subject.

Experience indicates, however, that these definitions are not just idle chatter for semanticists. They represent separate world views that lead managers to significantly different behaviors and levels of effectiveness. The rationalist assumption is widespread and often results in a particular view of employees. For example, consider the key assets of an organization seen as a rational system: capital, equipment, information systems, and people. Which is the least logical link in this chain of resources? The answer is people, the human resource.

In this world view, people become problems and costs. Nurses have been known to say, "This would be a great place to work if it weren't for the damned patients." Teachers echo this sentiment except students become the centerpiece. Exhibit 11 represents a story popular among plant managers who see people mainly as a source of irrationality causing endless difficulties that slow down production.

A Rationalist's Dream

A plant manager of about 3,000 employees was taking some visitors on a tour. He was boasting of recent additions in robotics. " I hope for the day," he said, "when this entire plant will be run with just a man and a dog. The job of the man will be to feed the dog. And the job of the dog will be to keep the man's hands off the damn controls."

---

exhibit 11

Political Savvy

These managers push for automation as the way to make organizations rational. It's easy for anyone who has had to manage sticky employee problems to empathize with this simplistic perspective.

Viewing people as problems blocking organizational productivity makes it difficult to see them as solutions to gaining a competitive advantage. As one CEO of a plastics firm commented on his technically oriented head of manufacturing, "The trouble with Hank is that he has an irrational passion for dispassionate rationality. Organizations and people are complex, but he doesn't seem to even want to understand that. Too bad, with his knowledge of the business he could have made one hell of a future president."

While not as popular as the first definition, the second organizational definition seems a better match for the realities of organizational life. When organizations are viewed as human systems, people represent the source of profitability rather than a necessary evil. Politically savvy individuals implicitly seem to view organizations from this perspective. It becomes common sense to work the human system with as much attention as the technical system.

The productive beauty of machines is that they have only one agenda—that set by the designers. A copy machine in the legal section doesn't plot how to get closer to the snazzy Xerox down the hall in human resources. The computer in the finance department doesn't worry about competing with the one in the research and development laboratory. The drill press on the shop floor doesn't try to protect its job security by threatening to pull its own plug and go on strike.

The human resource is the only resource with multiple public and private agendas, all of which change over time. These multiple agendas make people the most volatile part of the company's total asset mix. Volatility is one of the reasons technically oriented managers, who understand single agenda resources, find people so vexing to manage. Their primary response is often to control rather than lead the human element. As one superintendent in a computer plant summed up his beliefs, "I don't care what all the management experts say; when you get right down to it, people are irrational. If you don't control them from the start, they quickly get off the track and chaos results." When one is not used to managing resources with multiple agendas, control is a natural response to prevent disorder. While savvy managers favor control at strategic points, the notion of heavy-handed control is generally not associated with being politically savvy.

The Savvy generally take a different approach. Since they view organizations as primarily human systems, they start by assuming that multiple diverse agendas pervade the organization. Although they don't like the disorder, they do like the energy. "Sure this place is like a giant soap opera," commented a CEO in an insurance firm, "How could it not be with talented, ambitious people who have complicated lives. But the trick is to tap into it, release and align all that energy into productive work. It's not easy, but I'm having a hell of a good time." Or, as a department head remarked, "Yes, people are not entirely rational but neither is the creative process, which is where our best products come from. Neither are emotions, the source of the commitment to excellence which keeps our employees going that extra mile for our customers."

The rational manager relies on traditional carrot-and-stick approaches for motivation. This orientation runs the greatest risk during times of organizational change. To change a rational system, one needs to explain the rational reason for the change and put in the appropriate rational rewards and penalties to ensure implementation. However, human system change often doesn't follow rational rules. Just ask someone who has attempted to make a major personal change. Anyone who has, for example, tried to lose weight, quit smoking, or stop gambling knows the rational component is necessary, but not sufficient. Most people who smoke or are overweight have made the rational decision to change based on the overwhelming scientific data on health hazards. Yet, no matter how much logical data there is, something additional is frequently needed for a person's behavior to actually change even when all the rational incentives are in place.

Since organizations are complex collections of many human systems, purely rational approaches to change often run aground. When desired outcomes are not achieved, it is frequently chalked up to organization politics. To the Savvy, organization politics is just another label for human nature.

Managers who stay out of organization politics because of the rational block sometimes miss a critical point. The politically Savvy get involved for the very purpose of making the organization decisions more rational! Since they are pragmatists and realize that human nature is only partly rational, they become active in organization politics precisely to prevent the more dysfunctional irrational aspects of human nature from distorting the decision-making process. Exhibit 12 summarizes one highly successful executive's development that led to busting through the rational block.

Journey from Novice to Master Manager

It was awful. Everything was always changing and nothing ever seemed to happen. The people above me would sit around forever and talk about things. The technically right answer didn't matter. They were always making what I thought were wrong decisions, and when I insisted on doing what was right, they got pissed off and would ignore what I was saying. Everything was suddenly political. They would worry about what everyone was going to think about every issue. How you looked, attending cocktail parties—that stuff to me was unreal and unimportant. I went through five and a half terrible years. I occasionally thought I had reached my level of incompetence, but I refused to give up. In the end, the frustration and pain turned out to be a positive thing because it forced me to consider some alternative perspectives. I eventually learned that there were other realities beside the technical reality. I discovered perception and long time lines. At higher levels what matters is how people see the world, and everyone sees it a little differently. Technical facts are not as available or as important. Things are changing more rapidly at higher levels; you are no longer buffered from the outside world. Things are more complex, and it takes longer to get people on board. I decided I had to be a lot more receptive and a lot more patient. It was an enormous adjustment, but then things started to change. I think I became a heck of a lot better manager.

—Robert E. Quinn, *Beyond Rational Management*

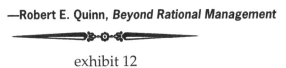

exhibit 12

A Definition of Organization Politics

Politics is a fact of organizational life. If one can get past the political blind spot by breaking through the moral and rational blocks then one can choose to move into the active portion of the Political Style Grid. Politically active managers can use organization politics for good or ill. Any working definition of organization politics should contain these possibilities. While there have been many definitions over the years, most boil down to self-interest and how it plays out in the organization. The Interest Grid in exhibit 13 portrays the two major elements contained in most definitions of organization politics: self-interest and the organization's interest.

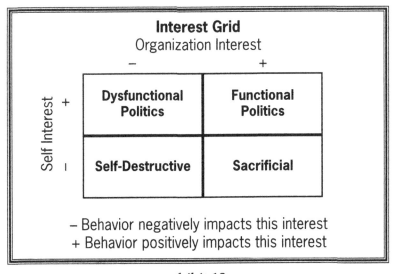

exhibit 13

Political Savvy

The upper left-hand corner is where the feared Machs dwell. While going to great lengths to appear to benefit the organization' their major interest is in advancing their personal ambitions. Dysfunctional politics occurs when individuals promote their own interests at the expense of the organization. An example is a manager who agrees with the boss's idea while knowing it's ill-founded. Approval by a superior is gained at the eventual expense of the organization.

The upper right corner, functional politics, signifies actions primarily aimed at benefiting the organization. This area is where the politically Savvy dwell. It represents the ideal of the capitalist system and the goal of effective organization design. Organizations within the capitalist system are set up under the principle that the best way to achieve one's own interests is to benefit the whole. Dysfunctional politics is based upon self-interest as the driving force, while functional politics is motivated by enlightened self-interest. The Savvy operate chiefly in the functional politics zone. Being savvy doesn't mean being dumb about one's own career. It does mean putting the organization's interests first.

While the active players generally stay in the upper two quadrants, there are times when they can end up in the bottom two. When conflicts arise between organization and personal interests, savvy players may take the "sacrificial hit," giving up some of their own personal agenda for the good of the organization. While it may sound noble—and sometimes it actually is—it is also smart. Since the orientation of the Savvy is to do what they think is right for the organization, it is natural for them to put the interests of the organization first. They also know that a reputation for putting aside personal agendas builds credibility. However, few savvy individuals spend a great deal of time operating in this area. If they do, they eventually burn out or develop martyr syndromes. Now, the Machs love martyrs. A skillful appeal to the martyrs' nobility can turn them into kamikazes for the Machs' own personal agendas.

Very few people last long in the bottom left corner.

The Political Blind Spot

Sometimes when Machs are losing, they may slip into this area. As one angry manager who didn't receive an important promotion remarked, "If I'm going to go down, I'm going to take the whole place with me." Generally, individuals who enter this quadrant are deeply frustrated by some aspect of their organizational or personal life and begin to engage in self-destructive behavior.

The Interest Grid is similar to the Political Style Grid in chapter 2. They both characterize certain aspects of political behavior. The Styles Grid focused on values and activeness, while the Interests Grid addresses goals and motivation. The Machs occupy the upper left portion in both grids and the Savvy occupy the upper right portions. Together the grids allow one to make crucial distinctions between players in the political arena.

Enough groundwork has been laid to develop a working definition of organization politics (see exhibit 14). This definition is neither elegant nor surprising. In fact, it's rather mundane. However, it does make several key points to build upon when the strategy and tactics of the Savvy are discussed in chapters 6-11.

Organization Politics
How power and interests play out in the organization

exhibit 14

First, it's stated in neutral rather than negative terms like some definitions of organization politics. This aspect is important because negative definitions trigger the political blind spot that prevents otherwise talented individuals from developing their savvy skills. Second, the definition allows for all twelve styles of the Political Style Grid. Third, it zeros in on the two major components of all savvy strategies: (1) the power or influence of the people involved and (2) their interests or agendas, both personal and organizational. Fourth, it implies that to understand the politics in one's own organization, one needs to focus on how these sets of agendas play out or interact.

The Machs versus the Savvy: Distinguishing Characteristics

By now it should be clear that organization politics is a double-edged sword. One edge, used by the Machs, cuts out the organization's vitality as people see rewards go to slick manipulators. The other edge, used by the Savvy, can slice through bureaucracy, turfs, and favoritism to ensure that the organization's interests are best served.

Both the Machs and the Savvy are in the upper portion of the Political Style Grid. That is, at least for certain issues, they both have decided to be active players and jump into the political arena. They both go beyond their official job descriptions to affect key organizational decisions. They both work the informal as well as the formal organization in their attempts to impact the situation. In other words, the Machs and the Savvy often look alike.

The question naturally arises that, if one avoids the political blind spot by overcoming the moral and rational blocks to becoming active, how does one get perceived as a Savvy rather than as a Mach? Since they are similar in that they are quite active, how do others tell them apart?

Machiavellian versus Savvy Distinctions	
Reputation is based upon the manner in which the common characteristics are played out.	
Machiavellian	**Savvy**
• Manipulates	• Influences
• Creates Losers	• Creates Winners
• Lone Wolf	• Team Player
• Power for Its Own Sake	• Power to Get Things Done
• Boot Licking, Brownnosing	• Respect, Choosing Shots
• Promotion as Goal	• Promotion as Outcome
• Hidden Agendas	• Open Agendas
• Word as Tool	• Word as Bond
• Calculating	• Strategist
• Gossip	• Relay
• Politician	• Statesman
• Takes Credit	• Spreads Credit

exhibit 15

While the Machs and the Savvy are both active players, what separates them is their intentions, behaviors, and results. The Machs have little difficulty in resorting to manipulation. The Savvy avoid this form of influence. The Savvy have a deeply held belief that the basic role of the organization is to align the interests of individuals with those of the organization. Therefore the Savvy try to find the win-win in the situation. The

Political Savvy

Machs, on the other hand, frequently have a "pike fish assumption" that if someone wins, someone else has to lose. They often spend their time sizing up the situation and calculating how to raise their image or lower someone else's. The Savvy also spend time sizing up the situation but in order to use influence openly for their point of view.

The Machs frequently end up as lone wolves since they don't want their true ambitions known. The Savvy are frequently team players and build alliances. They actively try to gain support because they know it takes a critical mass of agreement to make their agenda work. The Savvy are also more interested in influence than absolute control. They see power as a means to get something done. The Machs view power as an end in itself akin to the quote from Orwell's 1984 in exhibit 4. Both the Machs and the Savvy can be seen deferring to higher authority at times. The Machs engage in such behavior to gain the favor of those in power. The Savvy do so to show respect and to avoid winning small battles that might lose the larger war.

The Savvy care about their careers. They enjoy advancement as much as anyone. However, they often view promotion more as an outcome of making a contribution to the company than as the primary goal. Machs see the process in reverse. Whatever it takes to climb the next rung on the success ladder is fair game. It can mean benefiting the organization or it can mean undermining an internal competitor, or both. Because the Machs are willing to utilize a wide variety of means to advance their ambition, many of their agendas are hidden. The Savvy have less to hide and therefore most of their agendas are open and public. Since they honestly believe in and care about their proposals, they have less reason to hide their motives. Because the Savvy see the positive side of politics, they have no need to deny their political activity or develop a political blind spot to protect their self-image.

Everything is a tool to Machs including their word. They use a promise as a stratagem if they believe it will divert potential opposition for a little while. This was Hitler's basic motive in signing a nonaggression pact with Russia. For the Savvy,

The Political Blind Spot

integrity is its own reward, and they know efficiency increases when their word is taken as their bond. The Savvy understand the importance of building trust in organizations, and they go out of their way to keep their commitments.

Both the Savvy and the Machs think about how to navigate their agendas through the organization. For the Savvy, this means strategizing how to align the diverse interests of the key individuals involved. For the Machs it means calculating the personal gains and losses of each move.

The organizational grapevine is an important conduit for the Savvy and the Machs alike. The Machs have a greater tendency to use it as a means of spreading potentially damaging information through informal channels. The Savvy use it as a source of information for how the organization perceives what's going on. They also use it to spot potential obstacles and opportunities.

Both use finesse as a prime tool to achieve their objectives. The Machs can come across like the negative stereotype of politicians. They talk about motherhood and apple pie, dance away from the real issues, and do whatever is expedient. The Savvy address conflicts diplomatically in ways that avoid damage to others' self-esteem. They act like statesmen who encourage people to rise above their selfish interests by appealing to an enlightened self-interest that benefits each to some degree. There are other distinctions, but these should help illuminate key differences between the Machs and the Savvy. The more people come across as working for the best interest of the business as a whole, and the more they spread credit instead of grabbing it, the more likely they will be seen as a Savvy instead of a Mach.

While the real world is full of blends, the bad-guy, good-guy extreme stereotyping has been deliberate. It dramatizes the point that there is a way to be an active player in organization politics without becoming manipulative and sacrificing one's personal integrity. It may not be easy, but it is possible. Some savvy individuals carry it even further. As one savvy manager commented, "It's not only possible, it's my job to develop these skills in myself and in my subordinates."

SUMMARY OF PART ONE

The greatest discovery of our generation is that attitude is the most important ingredient in changing behavior.

—Henry James, *Selected Letters*

Part one placed strong emphasis on examining assumptions about political style and overcoming the political blind spot. This emphasis may seem unnecessary to some. In fact, my own initial stance was to regard these issues as important but not essential in becoming more savvy. After all, the behaviorists in psychology have shown that the reverse of James's statement can also be true. Experience over the years indicates otherwise when it comes to political savvy, however. More important than strategy skills, interpersonal abilities, and intellectual capacity (which are all significant in becoming savvy) was the *attitude* of those identified as highly savvy. This attitude, although generally implicit and unconscious, is a compilation of the assumptions, values, and beliefs about organizations, covered in part one. It is found in just a small percentage of all management. This experience leads to the following premise about leadership behind-the-scenes.

The savvy attitude is the single most important ingredient in becoming politically savvy.

With this attitude, characterized in exhibit 17, several of the skills and strategies start to develop naturally. Without it, the individual either never becomes active or turns into a Mach. Understanding the Savvy attitude and what blocks its development, therefore, is critical to developing savvy skills in managers.

> **Characteristics of a Political Savvy Individual**
>
> Chooses to become an active, ethical player:
> - Puts the organization first
> - Believes in and cares about the issue at hand
> - Sees a career as an outcome rather than a goal
> - Plays above board
> - Legitimizes the task: avoids the political blind spot.

exhibit 16

The basic message is: choose to become an active player in the human system, put the organization first, play above board, and most important of all, *legitimize the task*. That is, accept the fact that human nature and organization politics are inseparable. Go beyond strict job descriptions and take some responsibility for the organization as a whole.

CHAPTER NOTES

[1] David C. McClelland, *Power: The Inner Experience* (New York: Wiley, 1975), 254.

[2] According to legend, the person who could unravel this knot would become ruler of all of Asia.

PART TWO

Systematically Understanding the Political Lay of the Land

You can't tell the players without a scorecard.

—Vendor at Yankee Stadium

Chapter 4

A CASE EXAMPLE: THE FUTURE OF THE MILFORD STEEL COMPANY

Management is itself a political activity.

—Jeffrey Pfeffer, *Power in Organizations*

Once a politically savvy orientation has been legitimized, the next question managers typically ask is, "Now what?" The savvy attitude allows one to enter the jungle of organization politics with a sense of adventure and integrity. The next step is to develop a pragmatic way of mapping out the political jungle in particular settings.

Many of the strategies and techniques are difficult to discuss without concrete examples to illustrate them. The case now presented is based upon an actual company. It will be used throughout the rest of the book as a reference point. The case takes place in a manufacturing setting. However, the issues are directly relevant to service and non-profit organizations.

The case describes a real situation in which savvy skills

Political Savvy

were essential in making changes at a crucial point in a company's history. Key features have been disguised to protect the innocent and the guilty. Test your political savvy by developing your own solution. Delving into a particular situation may seem onerous at first glance but hang in there. The investment will bring high returns in the form of specific techniques and strategies.

••••••

THE CHROMIUM PROJECT: "TIPTOEING THROUGH THE POLITICAL MINEFIELD"

The Situation: It's Monday afternoon. On Friday at 2:00 p.m., the top managers of the Milford Steel Company will meet to decide whether to invest the major portion of the capital budget in a new product line of chromium steel. Milford's CEO is undecided. The members of his top management team are each examining the issue from their particular perspectives. He will let their opinions determine the decision.

The Key Players:
Craig Louton—vice president of Legal, 48 years old; tenure: 3 years

Tom Ansell—vice president of Manufacturing, 55 years old; tenure: 28 years

Alice Johnson—vice president of Marketing, 41 years old; tenure: 1 year

Owen Farthing—vice president of Finance, 59 years old; tenure: 30 years

Bill Stanton—vice president of Research and Development (R&D); 60 years old, tenure: 33 years

A Case Example

Task: Alice Johnson wants you, as a part of her dedicated staff, to develop a strategy that will maximize acceptance of the Chromium Project at Friday's meeting.

Known Information: Alice and her staff have pooled together the following information related to the Chromium Project: The CEO values Owen's opinions the most, and Owen requires that the rate of return on the Chromium Project exceed 14 percent by the fourth year. He currently views the near-term financial numbers on this project as marginal. He has three children in college plus two sisters to support, and his overriding personal agenda is to succeed the CEO, who plans to retire in two years. Owen considers Alice a possible threat to his moving into this position. He also believes that the Chromium Project, combined with other proposed projects, represents an unacceptable drain on cash flow over the next two years. The CEO strongly agrees with Owen that Milford's cash flow must not drop more than 40% from its previous year's level.

Alice was hired by the CEO last year to put a stronger emphasis on marketing. After a thorough review of the trends in the steel industry, she originated the Chromium Project because she was convinced that it is absolutely essential to the long-term viability of the aging company. She knows that the project represents a significant departure from traditional steel manufacturing methods. This project will require three years to pay back its investment cost and then should have a 20 percent annual return on investment for the next decade. It is projected to drain Milford's cash flow by 30 percent from the previous year's level during each year of the payback period.

As Vice President of Research and Development, Bill

Stanton believes the new technology risks involved in the Chromium Project are within acceptable limits. His major priority is rebuilding the reputation of his department into a first-rate unit that is respected in the industry. He is currently looking forward to another proposal, the Tensil Strength Project, as one with good possibilities for his department to demonstrate its expertise. Bill sees that the Chromium Project has the potential for major involvement of his department, but he is concerned that outside expertise might be used instead to do the R&D work. The CEO values Bill's opinion but not as much as he values the opinions of the other executives. Owen believes Bill is too reckless and does not value his judgment. Although Alice is hard to get to know, Bill admires her and strongly believes she has the best interests of the company in mind. Bill owes Alice a favor for going out on a limb to back him in a key hiring decision that brought a topnotch engineer into the R&D department. Bill also knows that Alice has certain information which, if misrepresented to the highly moralistic CEO, would likely force Tom Ansell, the vice president of Manufacturing, into an unwanted early retirement. Based upon years of experience and perceived lost opportunities, Bill believes Owen and Tom are overly conservative in taking reasonable risks for the business. All things considered, Bill, at present, can't make up his mind about the Chromium Project and may just abstain at Friday's meeting.

As Vice President of Manufacturing, Tom Ansell tentatively opposes the Chromium Project. The CEO values his opinion second only to that of Owen Farthing's. Tom has pretty much topped out in his career, has five years until retirement, and wants to leave a company with a healthy future as his legacy. One of the reasons for his initial opposition to the Chromium Project is his view

A Case Example

that the new technology required for chromium steel production is too risky. For two years, Tom's primary interest has been trying to get enough of the capital budget and cash flow to build an additional traditional steel plant in Toledo. He knows that the original estimate of the cash flow drain for building the Toledo plant was projected annually at 12 percent of the previous year's cash flow and that the drain would last three years. When Tom went along with the Tensil Strength Project, the cash flow drain from the previous year's level was projected at 20 percent annually, for three years. Tom believes that the cash flow required for the Chromium Project and the Tensil Strength Project will not allow any near-term funds for building the more traditional manufacturing plant in Toledo.

Tom believes Alice is interested only in advancing her own career and therefore distrusts what she says to him. Alice knows for certain that if Tom and Owen both strongly oppose the Chromium Project, their opinion will rule the day. The CEO views Tom as probably too conservative about new technology. Alice is also aware that like Owen, Tom considers Bill Stanton as an oddball. On the other hand, Tom has complete trust and respect for the opinions of Craig Louton, vice president of Legal.

Craig believes that building a traditional steel plant would be a safe investment for Milford Steel. He is still trying to decide which way to go on the Chromium Project, slightly leaning against it now, but could easily change his mind upon further considerations. He has strongly held personal beliefs which include acting with complete integrity and in the best interest of Milford's long-term future. Based on Tom Ansell's opinions—and a bad initial meeting with Alice, Craig is not sure of her motives in proposing the Chromium Project.

Craig has just acquired convincing information that an impending patent infringement case will be tossed out of court, allowing Milford to use less-risky technology for the Chromium Project. Recent information about expected tax law changes in Ohio also has Craig strongly believing that the drain on Milford's cash flow from the previous year's level will be only half of that which was originally projected for the new Toledo plant. He deeply trusts Bill Stanton's opinions related to R&D and new technology issues. Craig is considering a possible move to head a larger corporation's legal department. The CEO greatly values Craig's legal and tax expertise but ranks his opinion below that of Alice, Owen, and Tom on basic, overall business decisions.

Alice is clear about her personal objectives. If the Chromium Project is implemented, she wants to remain the vice president of Marketing for at least five years. Otherwise, she will seriously consider moving on to a more progressive company. Alice is angered by Owen's and Tom's resistance and she knows Owen greatly distrusts her overall business judgment. Alice and Bill Stanton proposed the Tensil Strength Project, which they consider a desirable but not critical investment that would reduce Milford's cash flow 20 percent from the previous year's level, annually for three years. The Tensil Strength Project could be postponed for three years without much negative impact. Alice recognizes that the new technology needed for the Chromium Project could be developed outside as well as inside Milford. She also knows that the CEO values her opinion, but not as much as Tom's and Owen's.

• • • • • •

That summarizes the information put together by Alice and her staff. All the facts aren't known, and seldom can be, but

A Case Example

this group knows more than executives who typically don't legitimize pooling such information prior to a key decision meeting. Savvy approaches may not guarantee a solution, but they do up the odds that an influence attempt will be effective.

Developing a Strategy

Given this daunting amount and diverse mix of data, how should Alice approach Friday's meeting? After they have sifted through the available information, the initial reactions of managers to this case cover the full range from "Alice should leave because she is dead in the water with Owen and Tom against her," to "Alice should confront Owen and explain that she is not a threat to him," to "The situation is too complex so Alice should focus on making a solid presentation of the facts on Friday and hope for the best"' to "Alice has to play hardball and use the potentially damaging information she has on Tom to leverage his support."

Those who say Alice should leave often have diagnosed themselves on the Political Style Grid as being in the bottom left-hand corner where the protector, cynic, and fatalist styles congregate. Managers who believe Alice should confront Owen are frequently those with high moral beliefs. The advice to focus on a quality presentation of the facts generally comes from managers with technical orientations who believe organizations should be rational and logical. Those who advocate using the damaging information typically believe the ends justify the means and show strong desires to win what they see as a contest. They often hover near the upper left-hand corner of the Grid where the Machs hang out.

What about the upper right-hand corner of the Grid, where we find the Leader, Responsible, and Advisor styles? What approach do managers viewed as having these styles recommend? A consistent approach emerges when those perceived as politically savvy are presented with the Milford situation. Since the savvy approach is a little more sophisticated, a step-

Political Savvy

by-step explanation is called for. This provides the opportunity to introduce a powerful tool called the Organization Politics Mapping Technique (OPMT), which is the subject of chapter 5.

Chapter 5

MAPPING THE POLITICAL TERRITORY: THE OPMT TOOL

A picture is worth a thousand words.

—Chinese Proverb

The soul never thinks without a picture.

—Aristotle

The amount and complexity of information involved in any key decision-making situation can be overwhelming. It's impossible to formulate an influence approach without having some way to organize and picture it. Most managers intuitively organize information but risk being unsystematic and leaving out key pieces of data. The Organization Politics Mapping Technique (OPMT) was developed to capture in a more conscious and systematic form what the naturally Savvy do intuitively when they approach situations such as the Milford one.

Political Savvy

It's a concise and methodical way to size up a specific situation. The OPMT sets the stage for developing the practical strategies used in leadership behind-the-scenes. In order to generate these strategies one must first gain a sense for the political lay of the land.

The OPMT has three simple steps. It results in a map that collects on a single page much of the critical information contained in a given political situation. The first step is to ask the Five Basic Questions (see exhibit 17). The second step is to place the answers to these questions on the Political Data Sheet (see exhibit 18). The third and final step is to use the information from the Political Data Sheet to create the Organization Politics Map (see exhibit 19).

To demonstrate its use, the OPMT will be applied to generate an Organization Politics Map of the Milford Case, where the Chromium Project is the particular issue.

OPMT—Five Basic Questions Sheet
Issue: _____

1. Who are the key players?

2. What is their power/influence in the organization?

3. To what extent are they applying their influence for or against the issue?

4. How easily can their applied influence be changed?

5. What significant relationships exist among the key players?

---

exhibit 17

Mapping the Political Territory

OPMT—The Political Data Sheet

Issue: _____

1. Who are the key players?
2. What is their power/influence?
3. To what extent are they applying their influence?
4. How easily can their applied influence be changed?
5. What significant relationships exist?

Name of Key Player	Organizational Influence (1 - 10) Low High	Applied Influence (-10 0 +10) Against For	Changeability of Applied Influence ☐ ○ ▽ Low Medium High	Personal Relationships +/−

exhibit 18

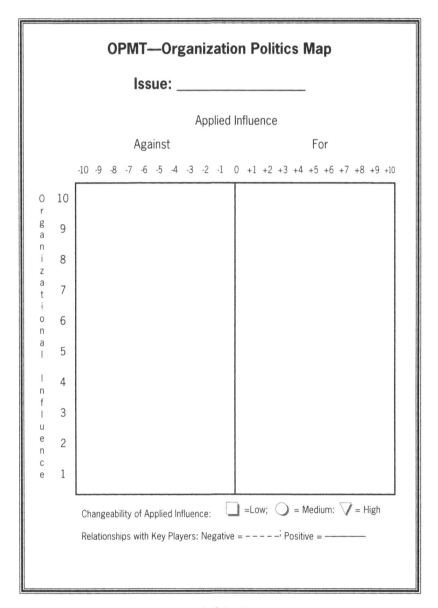

exhibit 19

STEP 1: SEEKING THE CRITICAL INFORMATION—THE FIVE BASIC QUESTIONS

The first question (exhibit 17) asks "Who are the key players?" Since the CEO in the Milford Case will let the five subordinates' opinions decide the outcome, the five key players are obviously Alice, Owen, Tom, Bill, and Craig. In practice, the key players are seldom as obvious, and answering this question for a particular situation often surfaces assumptions and other important information about the situation.

The second question gauges the general power and influence each key player has in the organization. The case contains information indicating that the CEO values each person's opinion, but in a certain order: Owen, Tom, Alice, Craig, and Bill.

Question three asks how much of their influence are the players currently using for or against the Chromium Project. Tom, Owen, and Craig are leaning against the project to varying degrees. As one would expect, Alice is strongly for it. Bill comes across as neutral.

Question four asks how easily influenced is each player's stance toward the project. Every one of the questions is subjective and this one is particularly so. From information given in the case, however, it's reasonable to infer that Owen's and Alice's stance will be difficult to change. Tom and Bill seem more open-minded and Craig could quite easily go either way.

Finally, question five asks for the nature of any strong personal relationships involved among the key players. Taking each player in turn, information in the case indicates that Owen particularly distrusts Alice and has no respect for Bill. Tom also distrusts Alice but has particularly high regard for Craig. Alice doesn't seem to get along with either Owen or Tom but has a good relationship with Bill. Craig has particularly solid relationships with both Tom and Bill, and Bill is poorly regarded by Owen but has a solid reputation with Alice and is trusted by Craig.

STEP 2: QUANTIFYING INTUITIVE JUDGEMENTS— THE POLITICAL DATA SHEET

The second step in the OPMT is to provide a quantitative feel for the responses to step one. Averaging hundreds of savvy responses to the Milford Case results in the estimates shown on the Political Data Sheet in exhibit 20.

The *organization influence* column starts with Owen, who has the most power but doesn't have absolute control (That would be a 10 rating). In this situation, everyone's opinion is valued to some degree.

The *applied influence* column shows that Alice is going pretty much all out for the Chromium Project at a +9 while Owen is digging in his heels against the project at a -9 and Bill isn't using his influence one way or the other. These directions and degrees of applied influence for each player can change over time.

The *changeability* column uses geometric symbols to signify the likelihood of a player's stance being altered. Owen and Alice are as stable as granite blocks in their position while Craig's opinion, which at present is somewhat negative, could be tipped easily. Tom and Bill could roll with the pros and cons of different arguments.

The *relationships,* column appears last on the Political Data Sheet and uses positive (+) or negative (-) signs to indicate where significant personal relationships exist among the key players.

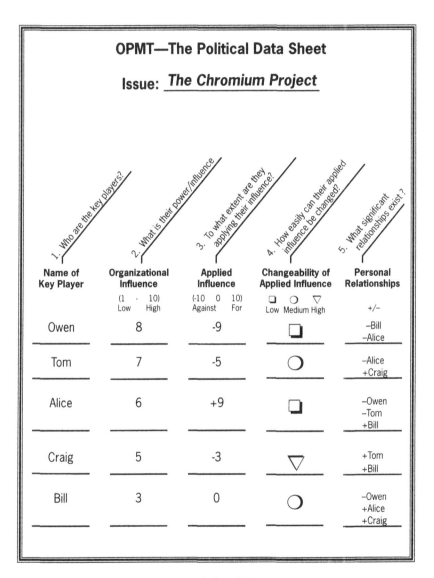

exhibit 20

STEP 3: MAPPING THE POLITICAL TERRITORY—THE ORGANIZATION POLITICS MAP

Step one surfaced the relevant information in a specified situation. Step two turns that information into quantified data points. In step three, these data points are graphed on the Organization Politics Map (see exhibit 21).

The map allows the complexity of the Chromium Project decision to be visually summarized. It displays the data in a form that shows key interrelationships. The vertical dimension of the map corresponds to the second column of the Political Data Sheet (exhibit 20) and represents the amount of overall influence a key player has in the situation. The horizontal dimension corresponds to the third column in the Political Data Sheet and shows the specific degree and direction in which players are applying their influence. Thus, while Alice has less overall influence than either Owen or Tom, she appears on the far right of the map because she is strongly applying the influence she does have. The geometric symbol enclosing a person's name indicates how changeable his or her current position is perceived to be and corresponds to the fourth column on the Political Data Sheet. As indicated previously, Owen and Alice will be difficult to move, while Craig's position is unstable and could easily be influenced. The lines between the players are visual displays of the information in the last column of the Political Data Sheet. They summarize the nature of any personal relationships that may exist and indicate who has personal credibility with whom. Thus Bill has a negative relationship (- - -) with Owen and a positive relationship (———) with Alice. Where no lines exist between two players, a normal business relationship is assumed. For Owen, as an example, the lines signify that he has negative relationships with Bill and Alice and normal business relationships with Tom and Craig.

Mapping the Political Territory

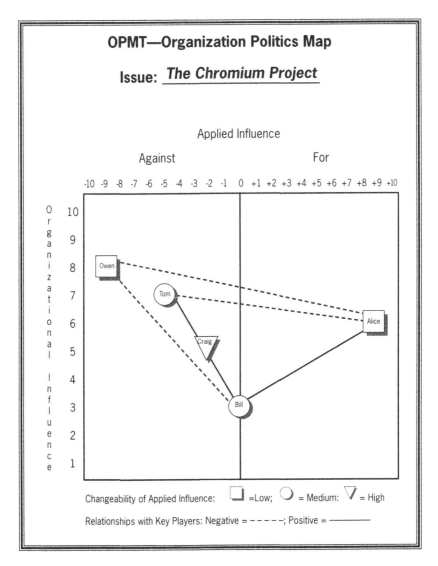

exhibit 21

THE ORGANIZATION POLITICS MAP OF THE CHROMIUM PROJECT

A quick glance at the map in exhibit 22 indicates that the situation doesn't look good for Alice. The most influential executives are against the Chromium Project, and she has a bad relationship with both of them. To make matters worse, there is no one else even in favor of the project. At this point, some managers typically respond, "I didn't need a mapping process to tell me that; it was obvious from the case. That's why I recommended she throw in the towel on this one." Or, as one manager put it, "That's why she should use the 'dirt' she has on Tom." The purpose of mapping isn't to illustrate the obvious but to put it in a broader, more complete context that may open up other avenues of strategy. Some specific advantages of the OPMT are discussed below.

Testing Assumptions

Most managers make assumptions about their own political situation. However, many of these assumptions are never made explicit so that their accuracy can be discussed. In the Chromium Project decision, for example, is Bill really the person with the least power or is that just an assumption that should be checked out? The mapping process brings many of the implicit assumptions to the surface where it is possible to consider and to test them. In this way, the picture represented by the map can be worth a thousand words. For a critical issue such as the Chromium Project, one major flaw in a manager's assumptions, such as assuming that Tom has little or no influence, can lead to drastic results in strategy. By displaying information in graphical form, the mapping process would make a mistaken ranking of Owen's influence relative to the other key players easier to spot.

Political Activity

The Organization Politics Map shows, at a glance, how static or dynamic the political situation is at any given moment. Many squares indicates entrenched positions, which will make influencing key players more difficult. A high percentage of triangles signals a very unstable situation where a comprehensive strategy can have enormous impact. A great number of players on the far right and far left indicates a highly polarized, very politically active situation, while one with most players near the middle shows a politically quiet situation—for the moment.

Directing Attention

The map also indicates where attention should be focused in the development of strategy. Triangles in the upper left portion generally deserve the highest priority. They represent powerful individuals who are now actively opposed to the project but whose minds could be changed by the right influence. Energy spent on these players has the greatest potential for payoff. One executive in an electronics firm observed such a change, which he described with suspicion: "The VP of Finance had been strongly against a certain decision when all of a sudden he did an 'about face' and decided in favor of it. I'm not sure what happened, but I think someone got to him."

Special attention should also be paid to any opposing player who has many solid relationship lines with individuals on the right side of the map. These solid lines indicate that there may be multiple ways to influence this person. The least effort is advisable for the square players in the lower center of the map. They represent relatively low-power individuals who have decided not to take a position on the issue at hand.

Identifying Coalition Levers

The absence of lines between the players indicates a normal business situation in which a straightforward rational approach has its best chance. A large number of lines portrays an organization soap opera, in which personality management and hidden agendas become key factors when creating a realistic strategy. Many dotted lines indicate a situation where straightforward rational influence will be particularly difficult because of the distrust and consequent distortion in communications. The more solid lines there are on the map, the more it will look like a spider web indicating greater ease of communication. It's the solid line pattern that becomes a cornerstone when constructing a viable strategy. Such a pattern could signify the presence of a strong clique or "old boy network" or the success of past team-building efforts. Breaking into this type of network might be difficult for an outsider. However, once one member of the network has been influenced, it should be easier to build consensus with the others.

Maximizing the Contributions of Outside Resources

Some initiatives for major change require the use of outside experts, such as consultants. One of the greatest difficulties for external consultants is that they seldom know the political context they are being asked to work in. When the internal manager has only an intuitive sense of the political terrain, a mutually frustrating and inefficient relationship can result. The consultant keeps proposing courses of action that the manager turns down because of a sense that they are politically unacceptable. If the manager has made an explicit attempt to map the political terrain, however, it greatly facilitates bringing the consultant resource up to speed. The map allows for a focused discussion of the political "lay of the land" and increases the probability that the consultant's expertise will be targeted for maximum impact.

CAVEATS ABOUT THE ORGANIZATION POLITICS MAP

The Map Is Static

The Organization Politics Map is only a snapshot of a dynamic political landscape. Any given map is just one frame in the ongoing movie of the situation over time. To maintain its usefulness, the map would need to be updated as major changes in the situation occur.

The X Factor

The map can be misleading. It can appear to contain all the relevant information, but in real life, there is always an X factor. That is, there are always relationships unknown to those creating the map. Also, the true influence of some key players probably will be underestimated or overestimated. While the map is a useful aide, it's important not to confuse the map with the actual territory one is mapping.

The OPMT allows numbers to be assigned with great precision. Some quantitatively oriented managers have assigned influence numbers that go to three decimal places. It is a common fallacy to equate degrees of precision with degrees of accuracy. An influence rating of 7.56 can seem a lot more accurate than a simple rating of 7. However, since one rarely knows all the relevant information, the X factor can make such precision frivolous and misleading. It's best to view the map as a clarifying tool rather than a precise depiction of the situation. The X factor is reduced to the extent that more points of view are included and an active information network is cultivated.

Burn the Map

Some managers who find the OPMT straightforward and

Political Savvy

systematic value the process until they realize what they are doing. They are putting down on paper judgments generally not made explicit in organizations: how much power various individuals have and who is for and against an issue. This realization often raises two concerns. First, what if the sheet should fall into the wrong hands? Careers could be jeopardized. Second, organization politics is inherently an underground activity. People generally know it's going on but resist legitimizing it and making it public. For these reasons many executives who want to use the OPMT encounter reluctance from their staff who feel awkward about adding their own viewpoints. As one manager expressed it, "It just doesn't feel right to be doing this." It seems okay to talk about this type of information in a bar or over coffee, but to actually put down on a piece of paper, for example, that a particular executive has the least power can put one ill at ease.

Some managers handle this issue by destroying the map once they develop it. Another alternative is to code the key players rather than use actual names. In any case, as long as paying explicit, systematic attention to organization politics runs counter to organizational norms, it is wise to restrict the OPMT to those with a savvy orientation, who have legitimized the task of working the human system.

Overmapping

Some managers who become enthralled with this tecnique start to use the OPMT for every project. While the tool is simple and flexible, it is best used for critical situations and major initiatives. Exhibit 22 illustrates some of the complexity that can be incorporated into an OPMT project.

This exhibit represents a major restructuring project in an aerospace company. The key players' names are coded with a capital C, representing specific executives who have a clear stake in the project. I's are the project team members. T's are

Mapping the Political Territory

Complex Organization Politics Map

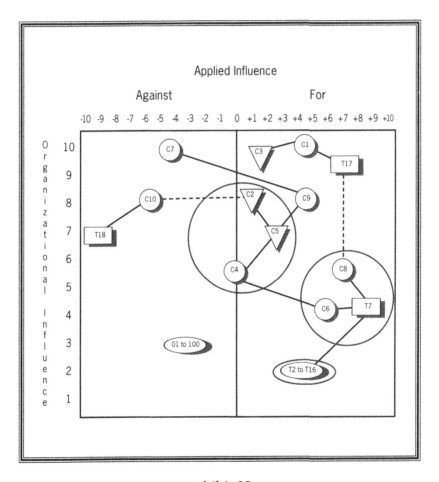

exhibit 22

members of the target group which, in this case, represents a department in which a matrix form of organization is to be introduced. O's indicate managers who are not directly involved but who control resources that could impact the success of the restructuring. An extra feature of this particular map is the addition of dotted circles around identified coalitions. In these circles are individuals who don't have much power singly but who could represent a major force if they collectively applied their influence to the maximum degree.

Complex projects and major decisions are the most useful situations to employ the full-fledged OPMT. Otherwise, one can get caught up in the technique to the point at which something akin to exhibit 23 occurs. Overcalculating creates its own problems and leads to a minutia mindset that can distract one from using simple good judgment. After all, the major purpose in creating a map of the political terrain in the first place is to help one step back and see the forest, not to step in and get lost in the trees.

Mapping Is Not a Strategy

A map of the territory is useful, but it does not tell one what to do. The purpose of the OPMT is to lay a foundation that stimulates more systematic strategy than would normally occur. It sets the stage for strategy development but is not a strategy in itself.

Mapping the Political Territory

THE FAR SIDE   By GARY LARSON

"Ha! Webster's blown his cerebral cortex."

exhibit 23

A Final Note on the OPMT

The OPMT has had some interesting results when applied to the Chromium Project in seminar settings. When the OPMT is explicitly used by groups of savvy individuals, they generally reach their strategy in half the time their intuitive approaches take. Even more interesting is that, when used by groups considered politically unsavvy, the OPMT generally leads them beyond their quick-fix reactions. Over two-thirds of these groups come up with the same strategy as the savvy groups. Asking managers to map the territory seems to bypass the political blind spot by legitimizing the task. Participating with others in a legitimized process helps to sidestep the technical and moral blocks to the point where the unsavvy have a way to bring forward their latent savvy skills.

PART THREE

Taking Action: Strategy Formulation

...[M]anagers, as strategists, must take into account the behavioral and political components of human action when they formulate the strategies that will ensure the success of the organizations they manage.

—Ian C. MacMillan, *Strategy Formulation*

Chapter 6

DEVELOPING COALITIONS

Never doubt that a small group of thoughtful, committed people can change the world; indeed, it's the only thing that ever has.

—Margaret Mead, *The Wagon and the Star*

Next is a small chapter about a large topic: forming coalitions. Even intuitively savvy individuals often overlook this critical element of strategy development. There are several advantages in forming coalitions and alliances; helping to manage the dark side of change is one of them.

Almost every manager knows about resistance to change. Some try to overcome this resistance by focusing only on constructive benefits of the change. These managers risk failure when they ignore the fact that change is an inherently destructive process. This point of view is aptly expressed by the old master himself in exhibit 24.

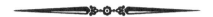

It should be considered that there is nothing more difficult to handle, more doubtful of success, or more dangerous to carry through than to initiate a new order of things. For the innovator makes enemies of all those who prosper by the old order while only lukewarm support is forthcoming from those who would prosper under the new. Their support is lukewarm partly from fear of their adversaries, who have existing laws on their side, and partly because men are generally incredulous, never really trusting new things unless they have tested them by experience. In consequence, whenever those who oppose the change can do so, they attack vigorously...

—Niccolo Machiavelli, *The Prince*

exhibit 24

Change destroys the status quo. Many bright stars of the past worked long and hard to bring about the changes that created the status quo. Like most of us, these individuals take great pride in their accomplishments and naturally have much invested in their own creations. A project manager in a mining company related her experience in dealing with the status quo:

The VPs keep telling us they want risk taking and innovation. I started to really believe them when they unanimously approved the new extraction technology. I went back to my project team and we started working out the details. It seemed like there would be smooth sailing. Then, as the project began to get implemented, something funny began to happen. I depended on the VPs' support for both budget dollars and expertise. They never retracted their approval of the project, but over time the dollars shrank and expertise became less available. I started to work 100 hours a week on the project but it still died from slow starvation. I think they began to understand how much the new technology would change the way they traditionally ran the company and it spooked them.

Unless one comprehends the destructive aspect of organization change, it is improbable that sufficient planning will be devoted to working the human system. The result is often frustration and cynicism, which drain managers' enthusiasm for undertaking the arduous task of progress. Overcoming the inertia of the status quo often requires some form of alliance for change.

ADVANTAGES OF DEVELOPING A STRATEGY COALITION

An ethical alliance—which is the opposite of a manipulative conspiracy—has several benefits: convergent validity, task legitimacy, enhanced ethicalness, and maneuverability.

Convergent Validity

Convergent validity is technical language for the fundamental issue in the parable of the blind men feeling the elephant. One felt a leg and said an elephant is like a tree trunk, another felt the side and argued that an elephant is more like a wall, a third felt the trunk and maintained that an elephant is like a snake, and so on. If they stopped arguing, they could combine their different perceptions and arrive at a more valid picture of the whole elephant.

The information on the Organization Politics Map is inherently subjective. Linking up with others who care about the issue provides other perspectives on key players, their influence, and relationships. If several views converge, there is a greater probability that the person's positioning on the map is correct. Consequently, a coalition brings much higher validity to the map than a single individual. Unexpected results often occur when other strategists introduce their perspectives. One manager in the lighting industry engaged others who were favorable to his initiative. He reported, "We had an unexpected result after discussing the situation. Bits of data were exchanged which raised some key assumptions. To our surprise, we concluded that, other than the head of Marketing, the person with the greatest influence in this particular case was actually the president's executive assistant! Well, let me tell you, it changed our entire approach."

Task Legitimization

Managers with the inactive political styles discussed in chapter 2 and those with moral or technical blocks often inhibit themselves from working the human system. The very act of co-strategizing can help overcome these inhibitions and legitimize the activity. Framing the task as influencing the organization in ways that minimize losers can diminish their ethical concerns.

Working on strategy in isolation seems to heighten concerns about becoming too political. In seminars where the Milford case was given as a group task, however, even those previously indicating strong individual reservations found the task valuable. Fears expressed beforehand, that the task is not appropriate, often disappear once one is engaged in such a group effort. As a manager from a Savings and Loan institution remarked when he started a strategy discussion back in his organization, "It was awkward at first, but once we got started the conversations flowed easily. There actually seemed to be some relief that it was okay to discuss issues we had all been thinking about in the back of our minds."

Enhanced Ethicalness

Concerns about being manipulative can actually become an advantage when working with co-strategists. Not wanting to be seen as Machs, people in a coalition often go out of their way to develop a strategy that is ethical, is above board, and has no hidden agendas. A forest products executive remarked, "Strategizing together not only brought in new information but it seemed in some way to check each other's negative tendencies. Every time someone would suggest an ethically questionable tactic, others would voice their concerns. I learned more about my own ethical orientation in that coalition than I did from any other single experience in my corporate career." Naturally, there is also the risk that the group could reinforce each other's unethical tendencies. Experience would indicate, however, that legitimizing the task, practicing openness, and involving others tends more to counter unethicalness than to promote it. Unethical behavior seems to thrive better in the dark of isolation than in the light of open dialogue.

Maneuverability

A coalition of like-minded people is more influential in making change than any single person. "Three small dogs approaching from all sides can keep one huge bear off balance and eventually drive him off," remarked a natural coalition builder in an industrial plastics firm.

Even if members of the coalition lack significant individual power, their common focus and collective action can greatly magnify their influence. Coordinated action in different parts of the system leverages each person's ability. As one frustrated U.S. general in Vietnam commented, "Despite our massive advantage in weaponry and complete air superiority, their tight cell organization structure—where each cell was dedicated, self-sufficient, highly maneuverable, and coordinated with others—proved formidable, given the nature of the terrain they knew so well."

The popular business press often portrays leadership as a personality trait of an individual. Consequently, the best way to make change is to find a Lee Iacocca type of leader to shake up the organization. In real life this is seldom the case. Even Iacocca may be more accurately viewed as the visible member of an active and dedicated coalition rather than as a lone maverick who changed the Chrysler Corporation. This is why Margaret

Political Savvy

Mead's quote at the beginning of this chapter is so relevant. Leadership in practice may be better characterized as a function to be carried out, sometimes in the spotlight and sometimes behind-the-scenes, than as a charismatic trait of a single person. The figure in exhibit 25 is probably a more realistic representation of how leadership occurs in today's organizations than the illusion that effective organizational change is the product of a great individual.

Alliances of ethical managers can play above board and still outmaneuver a Mach because Machs are frequently loners. They don't want their self-serving agendas known, so they keep their strategy cards close to their vest. Organized coalitions have the advantage of simultaneous action in different parts of the organization. They have more cards from which to create a winning hand and can keep even the most powerful Mach off bal-

"There are no great men, my boy—only great committees."

exhibit 25

ance. As an executive in an advertising firm which had just undergone a major restructuring put it, "The chief lesson I learned is that in times of change those who organize first, win."

DEVELOPING LEVELS OF COALITION

Since so much significance has been given to forming coalitions, just how do savvy managers go about it? For some issues, membership is straightforward. In the Chromium Project, for example, the actual strategy coalition was Alice and her staff. They strongly believed in the project and pieced together their various views of the influence elephant. The members of this coalition had two things in common: They were in the same department and each had a sincere belief in the project's value. The latter point is often more important in coalition development.

There are three major levels of involvement in developing coalitions: information, strategy, and action.

The Information Level

While this is the lowest level of involvement, it is absolutely essential The data in the Chromium Project came from this level. The wider the net of information sources, the more data one can capture about the human system and the more convergent validity the Organization Politics Map will have.

Most managers possess an intuitive sense of this level. Some call it their intelligence network, but most just know it as the informal relationships they've built up over the years. Savvy managers tend to be seen by technically oriented managers as wasting a lot of time socializing. In reality, the intuitively Savvy use hallway chats, office drop-bys, meeting breaks, and friendly conversations with diverse people throughout the organization for several purposes. One is that they may simply like people and another is to keep their information about the human system up-to-date.

Political Savvy

In his observations of how the most highly regarded CEOs operate, investigator John Kotter[1] aptly illustrates that the majority of their time is not spent in the classic rational activities of management, that is, planning, organizing, controlling, staffing, and measuring. Rather, these natural leaders focus on two activities: agenda setting and informal networking. They lead the organization by establishing a few key agenda items and then walk the halls where they "accidentally on purpose" bump into the people necessary to make these agenda items a reality. Likewise, the intuitively Savvy instinctively use Management By Walking Around (MBWA) to maintain their intelligence networks and keep them flowing with vital information.

All managers establish relationships over their careers. A difference between the Savvy and the unsavvy is that the unsavvy form fewer of these relationships. They are also more likely to let relationships fade when they move on to new positions within the company. The savvy managers, on the other hand, consistently seek to build relationships and then keep them up once they move on. It doesn't take much time, just a phone call now and then to ask, How are you doing? Also, savvy managers don't develop and maintain these relationships just to obtain political information, as a Mach might do. They recognize that the organization is a human system and they enjoy feeling a part of an extended team. A successful scientist at a research and development lab remarked, "I owe whatever success I've had to following a simple truth which my less successful colleagues seem to ignore. Underneath it all, it's a people business. I'll be effective only to the extent I know and care about the people here."

The Strategy Level

This level represents deeper involvement in a coalition and it usually includes fewer members than the information network. The strategy coalition digests the data from the information network to make accurate maps and generate strategy

Developing Coalitions

options. The most obvious candidates for this level of alliance are those who believe in the project and have strong stakes in the outcome. That's why Alice's staff was the strategy coalition in the Chromium Project. Each individual on her staff believed in the project and tapped personal information networks to create the material presented in the case.

Because many people develop political styles in the lower left-hand corner of the Political Style Grid and because moral and rational blocks are quite common, it is frequently difficult to get others to join in at the strategy level. There is no complete solution to this problem. However, a generic pattern can be perceived from an interview with a savvy manager in the navy who claims, as most naturally savvy people do, that it's just common sense. "I ask my people and others in the organization who believe in the change if they think the project is going to be a 'tough sell.' Many respond with a yes. I next ask them why they feel that way. Out comes all the data related to the forces in the informal organization. I then ask them what would have to happen for those forces to be handled. Before you know it, they start offering strategies or elements of strategy. I have these conversations one-on-one or in groups, depending on the situation. I don't understand why other managers find it so hard to strategize the politics."

By his attitude and approach, this manager finesses legitimacy as well as the moral and rational blocks. Step by step, he asks simple questions to which most people can readily respond. He doesn't start out by asking others if they want to be part of a strategy coalition. That approach would likely set off the rational and moral alarms. He just proceeds within the bounds of accepted behavior in his organization.

Managers who have been through some type of political savvy seminar have less trouble with the more direct approach. Otherwise, the strategy level of a coalition can often be created informally.

The Action Level

Planning strategy is one thing; action is another. Often those in the best position to develop strategy are not well placed to implement that strategy. For example, as the Chromium Project case unfolds it will be seen that only one person in the strategy coalition, Alice, actually took part at the action level.

To participate at the action level requires formal or informal access to the key players identified on the Organization Politics Map. The more the members of the strategy coalition have developed positive relationships with others over the years, the more they can take part in the action. Ideally, one would want a significant overlap between those involved in the strategy and those capable of being involved in the action. The greater the overlap, the greater the maneuverability because of the increased number of potential influence routes. As a minister trying to establish a new parish in her rapidly growing diocese put it, "We planned our approach carefully and we had enough support to blitz the bishop from all sides. There wasn't much he could do to oppose the move even though he wasn't a strong believer in it."

In summary, the information level of a coalition provides the raw ingredients for developing a strategy and frequently draws upon the most individuals. The strategy level generally contains a smaller subset of the information level and mixes the data ingredients into a viable strategy. The action level makes the strategy cook. There are significant benefits when the action and strategy levels overlap. A large degree of commonality is not as essential as it might seem to create effective change, however, as we will see in the next chapter.

Chapter Notes

[1] John P. Kotter, The General Managers (New York: Free Press, 1982).

Chapter 7

CHARTING A POLITICAL STRATEGY: AGENDA LINKING

Political behavior is an ability by organizational actors to accept and work with persons who hold different values to their own.

-Andrew Kakabadse and Christopher Parker,
Power, Politics, and Organizations

The basic steps in becoming more savvy can now be ordered as (1) consciously adopt a savvy orientation, that is, choose to be an active, ethical player; (2) form a coalition; and (3) develop a map of the political terrain. To some managers, these steps are merely preliminaries to the main event: strategy and tactics. Experience has demonstrated repeatedly, however, that if shortcuts are taken in the above steps, even the best intuitive strategies risk floundering on the organization's hidden political rocks. With that caveat in mind, we now move the focus to the cornerstone of all strategies for working the human system—*agenda linking*.

AGENDA LINKING

The primary components of agenda linking are: identify the multiple agendas, brainstorm the win-win possibilities, and build an action coalition.

Identify the Multiple Agendas

One reason technically oriented people can be so smart in their specialty and so dumb when it comes to managing people is that they prefer to work with single agenda resources. Machinery, technical equipment, and computers, as previously discussed, have only the agendas that were designed into them and follow the relatively stable laws of Mother Nature (e.g., physics, chemistry). People, on the other hand, have multiple professional and personal agendas operating simultaneously and follow the additional laws of human nature (e.g., psychology, sociology). These laws are not only more complex, but they are also less predictable than Mother Nature's physical laws. Consequently, it is a small wonder that the ability to work the technical system of the organization is not predictive of a manager's ability to work the human system. Working the human system is an entirely different ball game, one in which managers receive far too little training.

After mapping the territory, the next step is establishing as many of those multiple agendas as possible. These agendas can be discerned by various methods. One is tapping into whatever information networks are accessible to the strategists. Another is paying attention to how key managers behave in meetings. The issues people speak for or against indicate items in their agendas. Also, almost every conversation with key players reveals some clues about their professional and personal agendas. The identification of agendas is another area where multiple perspectives are particularly valuable.

The map in the Chromium Project showed a pretty bleak

Charting a Political Strategy

situation for Alice, but identifying the agendas of the key players can bring forth another dimension to the situation. Going back over the information provided in the Milford Case, exhibit 26 briefly summarizes the major known agendas of the five key players.

The Chromium Project: Agendas Summary

Owen Farthing—vice president of Finance

Professional/Work Agenda
- Wants return on Chromium Project to exceed 14 percent after the fourth year
- Wants to make sure cash flow doesn't drop below 40 percent from last year's level

Personal Agenda
- Most important, wants to succeed the CEO who will be retiring in two years

Tom Ansell—vice president of Manufacturing

Professional/Work Agenda
- Wants to build a traditional steel manufacturing plant in Toledo
- Wants to avoid risky technology

Personal Agenda
- Will retire in five years
- Does not want any other position
- Wants to leave a legacy of helping to establish a company with a healthy future

Continued on next page

Alice Johnson—vice president of Marketing

Professional/Work Agenda
- Wants the Chromium Project badly
- Recommends the Tensil Strength Project, but thinks it could be postponed

Personal Agenda
- If the Chromium Project is accepted, wants to stay vice president of Marketing at Milford for at least five years
- If the Chromium Project is not accepted, will probably leave the company

Craig Louton—vice president of Legal

Professional/Work Agenda
- Works for Milford's best interest over the long term

Personal Agenda
- Wants to act with complete integrity
- Considering moving to another company

Bill Stanton—vice president of Research and Development (R&D)

Professional/Work Agenda
- Wants to rebuild the reputation of the R&D department into a top-notch unit that's respected in the industry
- Pushing for the Tensil Strength Project, but could back off

Personal Agenda
- Takes pride in heading an industry-leading R&D function

exhibit 26

Charting a Political Strategy

Brainstorm the Win-Win Possibilities

With agendas of the key players identified, brainstorming by the strategy coalition is next. Strategizing starts by looking consciously and creatively for ways to link the various agendas. The goal is to develop a combination of agendas that favors acceptance of the coalition objective without severely damaging other important organizational priorities. This is the point where aspects of the technical system and the human system come together.

These dual aspects of strategy development show up vividly in the Chromium Project example. On the technical side, the agenda item concerning cash flow is critical. Because this is the only requirement laid down by the CEO and agreed with by the most influential vice president, Owen Farthing, it represents an agenda item that must be met for any strategy to be successful. There are two other projects under consideration besides the Chromium Project: the Tensil Strength Project and the traditional steel manufacturing plant in Toledo. The initial projections for the three were: Chromium Project, 30 percent drain on cash flow for three years; Tensil Strength Project, 20 percent drain for three years; and the new Toledo plant, 12 percent drain for three years. All totaled, the three projects represent a whopping 62 percent drain on cash flow, whereas 40 percent is considered the absolute limit. To do the Chromium Project at these projections would mean scrapping both the Tensil Strength and the new Toledo plant projects. While the Tensil Strength Project could be postponed, the Toledo plant is a major agenda item for Tom Ansell, and if he sides with Owen Farthing, the Chromium Project is dead.

However, Craig Louton's more recent information on tax law changes in Ohio reliably indicates that the projection for cash flow drain caused by the Toledo plant will be only 6 percent and not 12 percent as originally forecasted. This would allow both the Chromium Project (30 percent cash flow drain) and the new Toledo plant (6 percent cash flow drain) to be done simultaneously with a total cash flow drain of 36 percent, leaving a 4 percent cushion for the uncertainty of the projections. The Tensil Strength Project would have to be postponed, but since the primary backers of this project, Alice and Bill, do not see it as critical, it could be delayed. A delay does pose a potential conflict with Bill's desire to use the Tensil Strength Project as a means for rebuilding the R&D staff's reputation—a point that shall be returned to later. So it looks as though, with the right arrangement, the cash flow requirement does not automatically block the Chromium Project.

The other technical objection to the project is Tom Ansell's agenda item to avoid risky technology. The combination of two pieces of data from the information network might reduce the importance of this agenda item. One is that the CEO views Tom Ansell as too traditional and thinks he is overly conservative when it comes to new technology. The other is that Craig Louton, who greatly trusts Bill's judgment when it comes to new technology, feels assured that the outcome of a current lawsuit will allow less-risky technology to be used in the Chromium Project. This information might satisfy Tom Ansell's requirement to avoid risky technology, or could at least dampen his influence with the CEO.

Owen Farthing's other business agenda item requires the return on the Chromium Project to exceed 14 percent after the fourth year. This demand seems to be satisfied since the projected return is 20 percent after the three-year payback period.

Bill Stanton sees the Tensil Strength Project as a means to rebuild the reputation of the R&D function, but that project may have to be postponed. Alice knows, however, that the technology requirements of the Chromium Project could be met by expertise outside or inside the company. Using inside expertise could satisfy Bill's long-standing goal by using the Chromium Project instead of the Tensil Strength Project to demonstrate the value of the R&D department.

Craig seems more concerned about the company's long-term health than near-term profits. This fits with Alice's goal for the Chromium Project and thus represents a potential linkage point.

Next, it's important to examine the possible conflicts and compatibilities of the key players' personal agendas. The single most powerful agenda item would be Owen's desire to succeed the CEO in two years. From Owen's perspective, the Chromium Project could be an enormous success for Alice. He distrusts Alice and considers her a possible threat to his ambition. Owen could therefore see the success of the Chromium Project as a real danger to his personal agenda. Alice desires to remain the vice president of Marketing, however, so there is only an apparent conflict between their personal agendas.

The Chromium Project seems to fit, or at least not oppose, the known personal agendas of the other key players. It obviously fits Alice's agenda. If it succeeds, it will allow Tom, who gets his Toledo plant, to satisfy his desire to leave Milford with a healthy future. If the company goes inside for technology development, Bill's personal agenda is advanced. The project does not conflict with any of Craig's known personal aims.

At this point there are some rays of hope in what initially may have seemed like a lost cause for Alice. By sorting out and combining the various agendas, an approach compatible with most of the professional and personal agendas related to the Chromium Project seems possible. The Savvy realize the quantitative issues i.e. financial, technological, and legal issues are critical. They also realize that often it takes more than just getting the quantitative issues solved. Often it takes leadership on the qualitative side of organizational life to have a real impact.

SUMMARY OF AGENDA LINKING FOR THE CHROMIUM PROJECT

There are three major capital projects under consideration: the Chromium Project, the Tensil Strength Project and the new Toledo plant. All these can't be carried out because of strict cash flow requirements. According to recent information, however, the Chromium Project and the Toledo plant can both be done.

The Tensil Strength Project can be safely postponed. This allows both Alice's and Tom's major work agendas to be served while meeting Owen's financial constraints. The other potential block to the Chromium Project was the concern about the riskiness of the technology. This issue looks like it can be dampened by new information from Craig and the CEO's view that those concerned are overly cautious. The Chromium Project is not actually a threat to Owen's major personal agenda because Alice doesn't want to be president. Since Tom, Craig, and Alice are concerned with the long-term future of the company, that aspect of the Chromium Project fits their agendas as well. Bill can win both professionally and personally if the Chromium Project uses internal resources for the new technology. Hard work behind-the-scenes to link the multiple agendas in this way shifts the odds. There is now a potential action strategy that takes Alice's initially bleak situation and actually tips the balance toward the Chromium Project.

ACTION COALITION

Once possible agenda linkages have been brainstormed, it's appropriate to bring back the Organization Politics Map. With agenda linkages and the political lay of the land worked out, two of the three basic ingredients needed to construct an action plan are ready. Before we can discuss the third ingredient, credibility paths, however, we must take a brief excursion into the underground *chit* system of the organization.

The Chit System

Every human organization operates with some form of chit system. While difficult to precisely define, a chit is a type of unofficial influence credit. If bank checks are official financial instruments that can be cashed in to obtain material goods and services, chits are the informal vehicles that can be cashed in to obtain influence. Savvy managers are typically well aware of how the chits are currently distributed among the key players.

One can earn chits by several methods. In healthy organizations, the primary way to earn chits is through outstanding performance. Top achievers are frequently given more leeway in not following the minor rules of the organization. They can show up late for meetings, wear clothes a little different from the company standard, and generally behave in ways that would be frowned upon if their performances weren't so high. In essence, their contributions to the organization's success have earned them so many chits that they can easily afford to use up a few by circumventing the less important standards of the firm.

One can also build up chits by doing personal favors for other members of the organization. This is the primary way to accumulate chits in unhealthy organizations. As a result, the system runs more by favoritism than by merit.

Regardless of how chits are obtained, using them plays a key part in influencing decisions in organizations. As one executive in a legal firm remarked, "I had to call in a lot of chits on this one, but it was worth it since we did decide to move the headquarters to Los Angeles where our major clients are."

Chits are like influence in the bank. Savvy managers consciously build up chits in the system and then spend them wisely at key decision points. If one has no chits with another player, the likelihood of influencing that individual declines. At any point in time there is a natural debit and credit balance of chits throughout the organization. Knowing how chits are distributed at a given moment can determine both who has credibility with whom and how to use that credibility.

Follow the Credibility Paths

This is the basic rule of thumb in developing an action coalition. One standard assumption managers often make about influencing the human system is to go after the most powerful and influential individuals first. The Savvy, however, give greater priority to following the credibility paths, wherever they may start. They represent the yellow brick road in the land of the Savvy.

The Organization Politics Map for the Chromium Project is repeated here in exhibit 27, which displays the positive and negative relationship lines. The solid lines signify where the greatest personal credibility among the key players exists. A positive personal relationship can be based upon trust, previous history, or current chits. But in any case, it represents individuals who will be predisposed to listen to each other.

The only strong credibility relationship Alice has is with Bill. If the credibility path rule is followed, the action plan would call for Alice to go to Bill first, even though he is the least influential person in the entire executive team! She would use two points to enlist Bill in the action level of coalition. First, Bill owes her a favor from the past, and Alice could call in this chit to help gain Bill's cooperation. Second, she could offer to satisfy Bill's agenda by using his department rather than external expertise for the new technology needs of the Chromium Project. Making the Chromium Project a success would significantly increase the reputation of Bill's department in the company and in the industry. The Tensil Strength Project, which could provide similar opportunities to use his department, can then be safely postponed for several years.

If Alice is successful in winning Bill's support, the credibility path approach would have Bill—not Alice—talk to Craig Louton. Craig, while slightly leaning against the Chromium Project, is the least entrenched in his position, as the triangle on the Organization Politics Map signifies. He also has no identified hidden agendas, is a man of high integrity, and is primarily interested in the long-run health of the company. Bill can explain to Craig the benefits of the Chromium Project and assure him that the technology risks are not as high as Owen and Tom claim. Craig trusts Bill's technical know-how. He also has information that the initial cash flow and technical risk issues are smaller obstacles than originally thought. Craig therefore has little reason not to back the Chromium Project if it benefits the

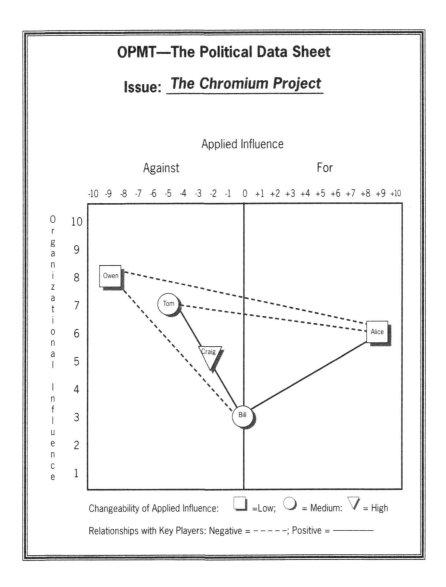

exhibit 27

organization's long-run health.

Next, following the credibility path, Craig—not Alice—would go to Tom, who distrusts Alice's motives but does trust Craig. Craig would link the Chromium Project with Tom's agenda of leaving a healthy company as a legacy when he retires. He would calm Tom's concerns about the riskiness of the technology necessary for the Chromium Project. Most important of all, Craig could show how the Chromium Project would not use up the cash flow that Tom needs to satisfy his biggest agenda item, that of building a traditional plant in Toledo. Sizing up everyone's agendas, Alice would have told Bill, who would pass it on to Craig, that she would be willing to back Tom's traditional plant and postpone the Tensil Strength Project. If Tom heard that from Alice, whom he distrusts, it wouldn't be as meaningful as if he heard it from Craig, whom he trusts a great deal. As indicated by the circle on the map, Tom is not that entrenched in his opposition and now has several reasons to back the Chromium Project in Friday's meeting with the CEO.

If well done, the action coalition now consists of Alice, Bill, Craig, and Tom. The primary block that could stop the Chromium Project is the joint opposition of Tom and Owen. That logjam has been cleared, and there should be enough support to have the Chromium Project accepted at Friday's meeting since Owen's financial requirements have been honored.

While the actual circumstances surrounding the Chromium Project were more complex, this account gives the basic strategy that was used successfully. The Chromium Project worked out well for the company: Alice stayed on, as did Craig, and Owen did become CEO.

Other strategy options. When given this case, managers develop a variety of other strategy options. Since there is seldom one right way to do anything, a number of approaches could work in any given situation. What follows are the four most common alternative strategies and the responses to them given by individuals identified as savvy by their peers.

Charting a Political Strategy

Strategy option one: Alice goes directly to Owen. This option seems to be a favorite among individuals with a strong behavioral science background. The rationale for this approach is to overcome Owen's resistance by having Alice tell him directly and openly that she is not a threat and does not want the CEO position. Sometimes such a direct approach can work, especially if Alice has extremely high interpersonal skills. Most of the savvy managers, however, rejected this option as too risky in the real world. The operational guideline applicable here is that truth told in a relationship of distrust has significant potential to backfire.

Owen strongly distrusts Alice. The effect of distrust is that communications are easily distorted and misinterpreted. Even though Alice is telling the truth, Owen could interpret it as a manipulative ploy. He might react with even greater suspicion and opposition to Alice and the Chromium Project. Since the map indicates both Owen's distrust (designated by a dash line) and an entrenched negative view (designated by the square on the "against" side of the map), most savvy individuals would avoid this option as impractical and having a potential to create an effect opposite to Alice's intent. This option is typically one of the most hotly debated issues when managers compare approaches.

Strategy option two: Alice talks to everyone. This option is most often suggested by managers who take a do-it-all yourself approach. Once the agenda linkages are developed, they think that Alice should just go out and explain the situation to her peers. Even if these managers agree that she shouldn't approach Owen, they still propose that Alice talk to Tom, Craig, and Bill. She can make a pact with Tom to trade his support for the Chromium Project for her support of the Toledo plant. Craig shouldn't be a problem because he has integrity and is interested in the long-term health of the company. Bill is easy to approach because of the credibility link where she has a chit she can call in, and she can use his R&D people in the project.

Savvy individuals generally rate this option as possible

but less likely to succeed than the credibility path approach. Since Tom distrusts Alice, he may be suspicious about forming any alliance directly with her, wonder what she is really up to, and increase his resistance. Having Alice approach Craig is less of a problem but is seen having lower reliability than an approach that uses someone he trusts.

Strategy option three: Alice talks to no one. This option is popular among managers with rational or moral blocks against working the human system. These individuals believe the best Alice can do is to stay out of the politics and focus on getting her facts together and preparing the best presentation possible for Friday's meeting.

Savvy individuals generally regard this option as feasible but naive and less likely to succeed. They assume that there are complex, dynamic interactions occurring between executives in most group settings. Or as one manager put it, "There is a lot of strange stuff going on when executives meet." When multiple public and private agendas are at issue simultaneously, the outcome of a new or controversial proposal becomes unpredictable.

Strategy option four: Alice uses the potentially damaging information on Tom. Machs tend to gravitate to this option, but even some other managers favor it as a last resort. Many savvy managers say they considered this option but very few used it as a part of their strategy, even as a last resort. Their primary reason for considering it was that they wanted to be aware of all the options, but their major reason for not using it was simply that it was unethical.

This option poses a moral dilemma between good ends (gaining the Chromium Project for Milford's future) and bad means (discrediting Tom). Managers who used this option typically cite an ends-justify-the-means rationale. The most frequently cited reason for making a choice against this option was the fact that the information on Tom was not true and would have had to be misrepresented to have impact. As one manager remarked, "I really couldn't have looked myself in the mirror the next day and felt good." Another factor sometimes cited is that the option is politically risky. If high-minded Craig found out about it he would likely withdraw his support from the project.

This option also has a more powerful limitation. Those who choose it stop thinking about other ways to influence the system and thus seldom reach the savvy solution. As one of them remarked, "Why think more about it when you've got such strong leverage on Tom to begin with."

Political Savvy versus Professional Lobbying

An apt question that often arises in discussions of the politically savvy is whether using political savvy isn't the same as sharp lobbying. Washington, D.C. is loaded with professional lobbyists and many people who take an active part in organization politics believe lobbying well equals being politically savvy. Lobbying emulates political savvy in that the best professional lobbyists legitimize the need to work the human system and try to do so in an ethical way—even though that may not be the public's perception.

Since many lobbyists are also politically savvy, making a distinction may seem like splitting hairs. However, there is an important difference. *One can be a great lobbyist without being politically savvy.* The distinction is critical because some managers who want to increase their political savvy pour their energies into becoming excellent lobbyists. Most dictionary definitions describe lobbying as using personal persuasion to influence those in power. This definition can create confusion between strategy skills and interpersonal ones. Many people who want to influence more effectively read books, listen to tapes, and attend seminars on interpersonal techniques such as active listening, interpersonal dynamics, and even body posturing. While increasing personal persuasion skills is quite helpful, it can mislead one away from developing strategy skills.

Among managers who address the Chromium Project, those who define political savvy as merely good lobbying skills frequently recommend that Alice go to each member of the executive group with the merits of the Chromium Project, and use interpersonal skills to overcome any distrust. They pay relatively scant attention to credibility paths and potential agenda linkages.

As a lobbyist, one can also fall prey to focusing on a single issue. While some of the best professional lobbyists do extensive agenda linking as part of their approach, many focus solely on the issue they are personally concerned about. They become expert on their particular cause and then use interpersonal skills to persuade decision makers of its importance. This focus can often mean that they spend little time understanding and linking their agenda with the agendas of the decision makers they seek to influence. In essence, they place their bets on raising the priority of their issue over other issues already on the decision makers' agendas. At its worst, single-issue lobbying is based on a win-lose orientation that fosters competition rather than collaboration among key players.

A similar risk in associating political savvy with lobbying is that lobbying is too often on behalf of special interest groups. A savvy orientation, on the other hand, means working for the best interests of the entire company.

While savvy leaders strongly believe in their own projects, ultimately they feel a responsibility to do what's best for the entire organization even at the expense of their particular issue. Assume that Alice found out that the Toledo plant was more viable and less risky than her own project and that cash flow requirements could not support both the Chromium Project and the new Toledo plant. Dysfunctional lobbying might argue for the Chromium Project even at the expense of what's best for the company overall. As a savvy leader, Alice would back off of the Chromium Project, at least for the moment. The Savvy recognize that their long-term effectiveness will be greater if they keep the total enterprise in view than if they work from the perspective of a single issue.

While lobbying and political savvy may seem similar on the surface, they can actually represent opposite underlying approaches. When lobbying focuses on promoting a single agenda at the expense of other agendas, it is primarily a "win-lose", "push through" approach. When linking together multiple valid agendas of others, the politically savvy focus on creating a "win-win", "pull through" approach.

The savvy orientation gives priority to strategy over interpersonal skills. At it's best the results can be quite dramatic. In the Chromium Project, the situation looks bleak on Monday, with Alice being the only one even for the project and distrusted by the two most influential vice presidents. The savvy strategy has her turning the situation completely around by Friday, with Alice talking to only one person, and the least influential person at that! This approach does not typically occur to those who equate political savvy simply with lobbying ability.

Political savvy strategizing does not generally produce such turnarounds as in the Chromium Case. (Alice was lucky to have the necessary agendas available to link together.) However, the Chromium Case does illustrate it's potential. Based upon years of experience, good political savvy strategizing probably doubles or more the success probabilities of an influence attempt, verses not strategizing. Ideally, of course, one would like a great strategy implemented by those with excellent interpersonal skills.

Definition of Political Savvy

Most discussions of a topic begin with definitions, yet, here we are in chapter 7 before political savvy is formally defined. If the journey has been long, it's because the destination is a bit unusual and a certain amount of territory had to be covered first. The definition is shown in exhibit 28. It does not appear in any dictionary. Dictionary definitions related to political savvy contain phrases such as *practical grasp* and *expertness in politics based on experience*. The definition of political savvy used here is in accord with dictionary definitions but is deliberately of a different character.

Political Savvy
Ethically building a critical mass of support for an idea you care about

exhibit 28

Political savvy is defined here more in operational terms. While not elegant, the definition states the specific components of the discipline that underlies the political savvy art form. It makes explicit the uncommon skill of the intuitively Savvy who often claim that "it's just common sense."

The use of the word *ethical* implies that a Mach is left out of the definition. This exclusion may seem arbitrary since clever Machs typically have great political skills. However, when managers were asked who in their organization was politically savvy, seldom did those identified as ambitious power seekers make the list. In practice it seems that individuals do distinguish between political savvy and self-serving, manipulative behavior. This distinction fits with the earlier point that while most managers say they abhor playing organizational politics, they would like to become more politically savvy. Managers considered savvy often follow an implicit ethical code. They live by it but find it hard to explain.

The definition is distinguished by the words excluded as much as by the words used. It does not include power or authority. Political savvy is not about acquiring power; it is about making an impact in specific situations. Political savvy as used here is not about the proper exercise of authority; it is about influencing those in authority. The word manipulation is excluded by the word *ethical*. The word *interpersonal* is excluded to avoid confusion with charisma or lobbying skills.

Political savvy has little to do with one's place in the hierarchy. The clerk who automates the mail room despite resistance

Charting a Political Strategy

may have more political savvy than the CEO who makes things happen by giving orders. In other words, anyone can have political savvy regardless of position in the company.

As to what is included, the definition involves *caring*. Caring is a more emotion based-heart-passion dimension. The definition also involves an *idea*. Ideas are more a intellect based-head-rational dimension. Democracy is an idea, so is a new computer network system, an inventory control initiative, or any innovation. Having passion for an idea that is good for the business is what allows one to care about something that is larger than oneself. Caring and passion also help give one the energy to go about *the central task which is building a critical mass of support* for the idea. Since one believes the idea is good for the business, one can be open and ethical about their agenda with others. Its hard to overstate that the starting point for the Savvy is caring about something bigger than themselves.

The tactics and techniques involved in managing the whole process consciously and systematically are the subjects of the remaining chapters.

PART FOUR

Tactics and Techniques of the Politically Savvy

The available evidence does not support the argument that power and politics lead to performance problems. Indeed there is some evidence that the reverse may be true. The Polaris (submarine) has frequently been hailed as one of the most successful and effective military weapons development programs undertaken in the U.S. The success or even the survival of the Polaris program was not assured at its establishment. It was skill in bureaucratic politics of the backers and managers of the Polaris project that largely accounted for its success. Even the famed management methods such as PERT charts and critical path analysis were, it was argued, used more for window dressing and to garner support.

—Harvey Sapolsky, *The Polaris System Development*

We are about to get down to the nitty-gritty of day-to-day savvy behavior. Let us assume that one has legitimized working the human system, decided to become an active ethical player, developed an information network, created a strategy coalition, mapped the political territory, and developed potential agenda linkages and an overall strategy for a particular situation. There are a number of tactics and techniques savvy individuals use to carry out and implement their strategy. The remaining chapters focus on several specific techniques useful in working the human system. We start with a brief chapter on organizational culture.

Chapter 8

101 WAYS TO SHOOT ONESELF IN THE FOOT: KNOW THE ORGANIZATION'S CULTURE

Having provided outplacement services for fifteen years, we are still surprised when we hear one of our clients say that his or her next employer shouldn't be a 'political' organization. We will try, of course, to help the client find the type of corporate culture he or she wants. But this particular request gives us a problem because we know it may be impossible to achieve.

—Lee Hecht Harrison, Inc., *Human Resource Executive*

There are as many ways to define organization culture as there are to define leadership. For the purposes of this chapter the operational definition given by a trucking company vice president will suffice:

Political Savvy

Everyone talks about culture, but it always ends up as a vague cloud that you can never grab hold of. To me, *"culture is simply the way things really get done around here."*

The official policies and practices prescribe how management thinks things should get done, but the culture determines what really happens. While there is a plethora of sophisticated theories about organization cultures from psychological, anthropological, and sociological perspectives, exhibit 29 captures the essence of organization culture in action.

THE FAR SIDE ©1985 UNIVERSAL PRESS SYNDICATE.
Reprinted with permission. All rights reserved.

exhibit 29

101 Ways to Shoot Oneself in the Foot

An organization may want to change into a more entrepreneurial company that takes greater initiative. It may, therefore, send out the call for employees to be more aggressive and attack the competition. However, it's the culture that determines if such behavior will be cheered or squashed in practice.

The first guideline in implementing a strategy is to learn ahead of time the hidden "Simon Says" rules that actually govern behavior. Then, unless the initiative is directly aimed at changing the culture, work with the culture to implement the strategy. Working with the culture is similar to cutting with the grain rather than against it. One reason for stressing this aspect of strategy implementation is that great technical talent is often accompanied by great egos. Managers with overly large egos are frequently less sensitive to the subtleties embedded in organization cultures. Often, they sabotage their own strategy by shooting themselves in the foot without even knowing it.

There is no generic list of foot-shooting actions because they differ significantly from organization to organization. In fact what works in one culture can backfire in another. Exhibit 30 displays only a short list of such contrary foot-shooting actions gathered from a wide variety of organizations.

Avoid Shooting Oneself in the Foot

- **Keep your peers involved from the very beginning or they shoot it down once the proposal is finalized.**
- **Don't let your peers know about the idea until you have all your ducks in a row or they move in and take it over.**

- **Avoid disparaging the past in presenting your ideas.**
- **Make sure you break with the past in communicating your proposal.**

Political Savvy

- Strike back immediately when someone attacks, or they write you off as a wimp.
- Never strike back in this department, or they think you're petty.

- If it doesn't have bells and whistles on it, nobody takes notice.
- If it is too flashy, people will ignore it as a fad.

- Never listen to what they say. The truth lies in what they don't say. Read between the lines.
- Listen to exactly what they say. They don't expect to have to say it twice.

- If you want them to do something, put it in writing.
- Never put in writing what you want done. People take it out of context.

- Don't dress better than the highest ranking person in the room.
- Be the best dressed person there if you want to be considered part of the new breed.

- Never be late for a meeting.
- Always show up about five minutes after the start of a meeting so they think you are busy and important.

- Skip the motherhood and apple pie and get to the numbers.
- Make sure you wrap the numbers in the company's value statement.

- If you want to make something happen, create a task force.
- If you want to kill a project, give it to a task force.

- Always start at the top with a new idea.
- Never go to the top with a new idea until the department heads with the resources to support it have bought into it.

- Once initiative has been accepted, "ride herd" on implementation or nothing happens.
- After you've got the idea sold, let go of it so someone else gets credit for making it happen.

- Make sure you indicate who received copies of your memos.
- Never indicate on your memos who you sent copies to, for it creates unnecessary suspicion.

- Social gatherings are a prime time for influencing executives.
- Never bring up business at parties because you get labeled as pushy.

- Always make an appointment when speaking with VPs.
- It's best just to drop by when initiating a new idea with the VPs.

- Innovation is highly prized.
- Couch your innovation in very traditional terms so it looks like a small improvement, rather than a radical idea.

exhibit 30

The next step in strategy implementation is to identify the foot-shooting actions in the part of the organization where the strategy will be applied. Among executives at Milford, for instance, it was unacceptable practice to have informal discussions over the telephone. As one of the managers commented, "We use phones strictly for business and not for chitchat." Consequently, it would have been unwise to attempt to use a telephone conversation for informal influence. It was also the case at Milford that executive committee meetings were very formal and polite, so it also would have been a mistake to attempt a candid dialogue about various agendas in the meeting itself. Alice knew, therefore, that she must act before the meeting in one-on-one settings.

An implicit norm develops in many organizations that managers must have all the answers at their fingertips. In such macho companies, bringing along expert subordinates to field questions would be regarded as a sign of weakness and technical inadequacy. In some firms, the use of humor is seen as unbusinesslike and unprofessional, while in others, not using humor can indicate rigidity and create doubts about the individual's ability to be flexible when the going gets rough. Group-oriented cultures can view one-on-one discussions prior to group meetings as a form of cheating. In that type of culture Alice's strategy might have to be significantly different.

All this means that a necessary step in implementing strategy is to uncover the informal norms of behavior that have developed in the company over time. Since Alice has only been with the company for a year, she is unlikely to know all the subtle rules that govern people's behavior. As she actually did in this case, she would need to use her more experienced staff to inform her of the faux pas she might inadvertently commit that would undermine her intent. The simple message, too often forgotten when attempting to change the status quo, is to be conscious of and work with the culture of the organization.

Chapter 9

BUILDING MOMENTUM

This new kind of business hero...must learn to operate without the might of the hierarchy behind them. The crutch of authority must be thrown away and replaced by their own ability to make relationships, use influence, and work with others to achieve results.

—Rosabeth Moss Kanter, *When Giants Learn to Dance*

For those who are still asking, "where's the beef?", this chapter has the most tactical meat. It addresses the nuts and bolts "secrets" of political savvy. Of course, as in most approaches to leadership and life, the tactics presented here are really no secret except to those unfamiliar with them. There should be practical nuggets for most people in this chapter. It can also serve as a checklist for you and your collegues to see if you are utilizing the full range of tactics.

Working a dynamic human system with multiple agendas requires a balance of systematic technique and artistic finesse. Organizations seldom change overnight and new initiatives require time to be properly understood and absorbed. Leadership behind-the-scenes entails building sufficient momentum for change to get over the hump of the status quo. The chief tactical issue in implementing strategy is building this momentum. Several tactics vital to the process are now discussed.

TACTICS FOR BUILDING MOMENTUM

The 51 Percent Guide

In the twenty years I have dealt with the good, the bad, and the ugly of organization politics, there is one particular tactical rule of thumb that stands above all the rest. If every other section in this book were ignored and this one tactic were the only thing remembered, then the effort of writing this book would have been worthwhile. For the talented Machs and the Savvy alike, this technique has best stood the test of time across industries, public and private institutions, and even most international cultures. It is the tactic of choice from diplomats to street gang leaders. Known under a variety of names and approaches, it boils down to the basic technique that is stated in exhibit 31.

The 51 Percent Guide

When dealing with a new or controversial idea, ensure that those who have at least 51 percent of the influence in the discussion (1) already understand the idea and (2) are willing to explore it further.

---

exhibit 31

Building Momentum

There are those who say this technique has been used throughout history, mostly intuitively. It has been argued that the Renaissance spread with the help of this tactic, breaking civilization out of the Dark Ages. Whether this is true or not, the more modest form of this approach has specific implications for working the human system in today's organizations. First, the 51 percent guide refers especially to new or controversial ideas. These ideas are most likely to challenge the status quo and consequently run the highest risk of being distorted and discarded for the wrong reasons.

The human communication process is not particularly well-known for either its efficiency or accuracy. In fact, when one fully understands the complex process of the sender encoding the message and transmitting it, and the receiver decoding it, it is a marvel that effective communication ever occurs at all. One doesn't have to get deep into the complexities to understand this point. Anyone who has played "whisper down the lane" as a child (illustrated in exhibit 32) has a good grasp of the difficulties from personal experience.

The New Yorker Magazine, Inc.
Drawing by Ziegler, © 1982

exhibit 32

While this tactic may seem like common sense, it is not common practice. Corporate graveyards are piled high with the bones of great proposals politely killed in executive committees. In many organizations it's almost standard procedure for those who develop a new idea to focus their energies on putting together a strong presentation and then to take it to a group of executives. The presenters hope their idea will be executed—that is, implemented. All too often, however, the executives do execute the idea—that is, they have it summarily shot.

Executives who want to resist change and defend the status quo generally have two aces up their sleeves when it comes to the high-stakes poker game of innovation: fear and finesse.

The fear card is put into play with remarks like: "We tried that before and it didn't work." "This sounds like the F project (most organizations have a notorious, capital F failure in their histories) and we don't want to go through that again." "I know an executive in another company that tried something like this and he said that, while it sounded good in theory, it was a complete disaster in practice."

More subtle is the finesse card. It gets played through comments such as "I like the idea but the timing is bad; maybe when things calm down a little...." "It sounds like an interesting notion but we don't have the budget for it." "The idea has potential. Let's assign it to a subcommittee for further study."

Each of these comments can be valid and each has a place in honest discussion. When played from the sleeve, however, both cards prematurely cut off dialogue. One executive in a plastics firm confessed: "If I don't like an idea but want to look cooperative, I immediately put it on the agenda for the next executive committee meeting. Given the dynamics of those sessions, the idea will likely get shot down or tabled and I'll still look supportive to the original proposers."

The 51 percent guide calls for a process more adapted to the realities of human communication and human nature. Its major tenet is to ensure that most of those listening already understand the basic idea and, even if they don't necessarily agree with it, are at least willing to explore it further.

This approach calls for step-by-step building of momentum. In its purest form, it represents an expanding spiral of influence. One person kicks off the approach by discussing the idea with a trusted individual. If both want to pursue it further, then the two speak to a third person. Then the three speak to two others. The five then speak with four others. Then these nine speak with up to eight others, then the seventeen speak with up to sixteen, and so on. The majority in each session is already familiar with the idea and is open to more discussion. In this way, the new idea is ensured a fair chance of being understood in every setting in which it is introduced.

The 51 percent guide calls for a more informal approach than one individual making an official presentation to a large group. The latter approach, while amazingly common, risks killing off the proposal.

The 51 percent guide can be met in several ways. In actual use, eight will not talk with seven and so on, as described in the purest example. The organizational world seldom works that way. It is more likely that one or two individuals will go to one manager after another informally until a critical mass of executives has been reached. A one-on-one process can be effective, particularly if there is trust and thus a credibility link between the two participants, as was the case in the Chromium Project example.

The benefits of the 51 percent guide are manifold. In a less formal setting an executive has an opportunity to bring out a broader range of questions and reservations than is possible in most public group meetings. There is more time to explain the idea than in any committee situation, where several questions may be fired at once with few receiving a satisfactory response. The open-endedness of informal conversations allows misunderstandings to be more easily corrected and since no decisions are being made there are usually additional opportunities for further communication about any reservations. An understanding of specific reservations can actually strengthen the proposal. Few change initiatives are born fully developed, and each reservation generally contains a kernel of reality that needs to be addressed by a successful proposal. The proposal can be modified after the conversation to take into account the executive's points. Finally, the informal setting provides an excellent opportunity to uncover the executive's other agendas, thus allowing greater potential for agenda linking as the proposal moves forward.

The Savvy are skilled at taking diverse perspectives and turning them into a single action plan. Such a plan represents an alloy of viewpoints far stronger than any one alone, created in a process akin to forging steel from its dissimilar base elements. A successful session enhances the proposal, and the executive feels listened to and valued (which is often not the case, even at executive levels). In addition, to the extent that the executive's own ideas or agendas can be woven in, another advocate has been created.

Thus far, the 51 percent guide has been pictured as somewhat of a vote-gathering process in which each person has an equal vote. As illustrated in the Chromium Project, however, executives usually differ in their amounts of influence. That's why the guide specifies 51 percent of the influence, not 51 percent of the people. If each person has approximately equal influence, 51 percent of the people can satisfy the guideline. If influence is unequally distributed, however, a minority of the individuals—say, the boss and a few key vice presidents— would satisfy the guideline even though ten or more executives might be present. The amount of actual influence people have in a given situation may have little to do with their official position in the hierarchy. Gauging someone's influence is, therefore, a subjective matter, but going through the Organization Politics Mapping Technique with a coalition of strategists ups the odds of triangulating a person's true influence in the organization.

The last part of the 51 percent guide stresses understanding and willingness to explore further, not agreement or buying in. The guide does not advocate attempting to create zealots and converts. Vocal converts are just as likely to stop the momentum process as further it because many executives are naturally suspicious of zealots. The 51 percent guide is designed to create a

Building Momentum

constructive balance between advocacy and openness. Final closure and agreement are not sought until one reaches the critical mass of managers necessary to put the idea into effect. If the idea has validity, the guide sets up a process whereby, to a certain extent, it sells itself.

When a final decision is made, the entire decision-making group can legitimately feel it is their proposal and not just the originator's.

This brings up another characteristic of the politically Savvy. To be effective at leadership behind-the-scenes requires relatively low ego needs. One who is truly savvy takes greater satisfaction from achievement than from getting all the credit. While the 51 percent guide provides a method for strengthening a proposal, it is also a mechanism for spreading credit.

When presented with the 51 percent guide, a frequent reaction is that of a manager in a cruise ship line, "I try to do that but generally I don't have time to go through all that rigmarole just to get something done." If the idea is an important one that a manager believes in, however, it comes near to proposal suicide not to follow the 51 percent guide. Another frequent reaction was typified by a sales district manager of a national shoe store chain: "It may make sense if you're a shmoozer but, personally, all this back-room dealing just to get a good idea across turns my stomach." This concern is typical but leadership involves going beyond business as usual and doing what it takes to initiate beneficial change. The tremendous inertia of the status quo, the likelihood of misinterpretation in any human communication, and the unpredictability of group dynamics in formal meetings make the 51 percent guide critical to working the human system effectively. Individuals ignore it at their own peril.

Use of Group Settings

The tactic for using group settings is an adjunct to the 51 percent guide but deserves its own discussion since a mixed message is often given to managers about the use of groups.

Managers who go through behavioral science training frequently leave with a strong impression that they ought to use groups more. Groups often come to better decisions and reduce errors. They also increase participation, understanding, and acceptance, which can result in more effective and efficient implementation of decisions. However, behavior patterns of those identified as politically savvy lead to the somewhat paradoxical conclusion shown in exhibit 33.

> **Use of Group Settings**
>
> Group decisions are essential for effective organizations, and group settings are often the worst places to make group decisions.

exhibit 33

Many managers find the statement contradictory at first. As one supervisor remarked, "If group decisions don't occur in group settings, where do they happen?" The scientific study of groups and their decision-making dynamics began in the 1930s. Groups were typically established in laboratory settings, often with people who were strangers to each other. Ninety percent or more of the group's interactions occurred in the group setting and many of the scientific findings about group dynamics came out of these studies. For the purposes of research, it was sometimes assumed that the group wasn't a group unless its members were gathered in the same place. In some cases even doing group business outside the group meeting was discouraged. This approach is very understandable from the perspective of research, particularly when openness and candidness were fostered as group norms. As a byproduct, some managers and professional group facilitators try to get most of the group's decision-making process to occur in group meetings.

The usefulness of such tactics is diminished when taken out of the laboratory and into the less candid and less open corporate world. In real organizations, the members of a given decisionmaking body often spend most of their time interacting outside official meetings. As a result, much of the group's life does not occur in group settings. It makes less sense to shove the bulk of the decision-making process into official meetings when this is the case. Combined with the inherent difficulties of communicating among strong personalities all with different agendas, savvy individuals know better than to try to force meaningful dialogues on controversial issues in a group setting.

Yet, group decision making is vital to organizational effectiveness. How do the Savvy bring about group decisions? For them, group meetings are the visible tip of the decisionmaking iceberg. They find group settings valuable for two purposes: initial exploration and official finalization.

Initial exploration. Using a group to explore possibilities can be quite productive at the beginning of a momentum building process. The key to making this group setting work is for participants to know up front that *no decisions will be made* at the meeting. Managers who feel a strong obligation to look responsible in front of their peers frequently adopt a judgmental and critical mindset when they believe a decision is going to be made. This mental set can greatly favor the status quo. When a final decision is the goal of the meeting, managers are often forced into a more conservative stance and a prove-it-to-me attitude. Freeing them up by announcing that the meeting is intended to brainstorm possibilities, not make decisions, often releases them from a critical mindset and allows them to participate in a more free-flowing dialogue.

A savvy manager who is a vice president in one of the country's top ten banks, tells how he set the stage for an exploratory meeting:

> *I was slowly forming an opinion that we needed to put more emphasis on expanding internationally but I knew some of my peers did not look favorably on the idea. At the next executive committee meeting I asked the president to put the item on the agenda. When that part of the*

Political Savvy

meeting came up, I started off by saying, "There are a lot of options we can pursue (implying he's a team player and working for what's best for the enterprise as a whole). One of them is increasing our emphasis in the international arena. While, as you all know, there are many obstacles, today I'd just like to get out some of our ideas on what it would take to make that option viable. No one is making any commitment and each of us can change our minds at a later date. For now, though, we are trying to tap into our collective brain trust for initial ideas. Jim (an executive he knows to be open), what are some of your ideas on the topic?"

His approach may have been overdoing it a bit but he felt it would fit well with the dynamics of that particular group. His comments are loaded with clear statements and other cues for an exploratory meeting.

After the meeting he reported that the president came up to him and said, "I don't know where this will all lead but we've never had a more wide-ranging, productive discussion on this topic." In an exploratory meeting, the ball ends up in the savvy manager's court, which is exactly the intent. An observant manager also gains valuable information about the political lay of the land from such a meeting. The manager should come out with a good sense of how hard a sell the idea is going to be. A great number of objections indicate a tough road but still can be used to develop strategy. Every objection or reservation shows a concern that needs to be taken into account or an agenda item of the manager who is objecting. In the Chromium Project, for example, either of two responses could be made to Tom Ansell's objection that the technology seems too risky. "Tom, your concern about the riskiness of the new technology involved has merit. What ideas do you have that would make that risk acceptable?" Or, "Tom, I understand your concern about the risks of the new technology. Is there another use of the capital that you would find productive?" In response to the last question, Tom may bring out his agenda for the more traditional steel plant in Toledo.

In a well-designed exploratory meeting, one either gets good ideas about making the project work or critical information for the Organization Politics Map and potential agenda linkages. Since no decision is being made at the meeting, one also gains much information useful in modifying future strategy. In Alice's case, however, the decision process had proceeded too far to hold an exploratory meeting.

In summary, there are two keys to an effective exploratory meeting. First, make sure that everyone knows ahead of time that no decisions will be made at the meeting. Group dynamics can change dramatically when participants sense a decision is about to be made that may upset the status quo. Second, avoid disagreements at this stage and value each perspective as it is brought out. Managers are often conditioned to use their expertise to show why a new idea can't work. The approach in an exploratory meeting is to respectfully respond to each such remark with a question like, "I can understand that concern. What are your ideas for what it would take to make the idea work?"

Official finalization. The other valuable use of group meetings is to make a decision final and official. The distinction between making decisions in group settings and making them final is important. Making decisions generally involves conducting the classic steps of decision making: analyzing the issue, generating options, and then choosing the most fitting option—all in one group meeting. Finalizing a decision means handling last minute obstacles, putting on the finishing touches, and attaching the formal organization stamp that makes it official and thus ready to be acted upon.

In the Chromium Project, Friday's meeting was designed to close on the decision. Alice felt that she needed to test out and build momentum for her proposal before then. Even after her efforts the project was by no means guaranteed. However, she felt comfortable that at least 51 percent of the influence was in the hands of those who understood the proposal and who were sufficiently equipped to explore its overall merits to the company (Alice, Tom, Bill, and Craig). Friday's meeting was essential to getting formal approval of the project. Without it, implementation could not have proceeded.

Using group settings to explore possibilities and finalize decisions implies that they are most effective at the beginning and at the end of the group decision-making process. It also implies that much of the influence process occurs outside formal group meetings. This is often the case in organizations. While it may disappoint those pushing for open group meetings and fewer back-room dealings, there are obvious reasons why this practice will continue. First, when group members spend most of their time outside the group meeting, it's natural to use this time to influence each other. Second, savvy individuals know that many agendas, both public and private, are involved. Therefore, it's unlikely that all the pertinent information will be raised in an official group setting. A CEO in the airline industry said the following about a meeting in which a potential merger with another airline was being decided upon:

> *The battle for and against became intense. Jim, my right arm and vice president of Marketing, was leading the resistance. He brought up one logical argument after another. I couldn't understand why, since the hard evidence seemed overwhelming in favor of the idea. It suddenly occurred to me that while I knew the merger would benefit Jim, he had no idea of what the personal impact might be. I then tabled the discussion until next week's meeting. Afterwards, I sat with Jim one-on-one and found out he did have concerns about his fate. I reassured him of my and the company's commitment to him. At the next meeting, he brought up a few concerns but all-in-all felt it was good for both companies, and he committed his support. The logjam was broken and the deal sailed through.*

Certainly there are times and situations where completing the entire group decision-making process from start to finish in one group meeting is appropriate. Savvy managers recognize, however, that group meetings are just the visible parts of the total decision-making process. They use group settings sparingly, wisely, and for specific purposes. The quickest way to jeopardize a new idea is to use a single meeting to bring up the idea for the first time, discuss pros and cons, and push for a decision then and there. Unfortunately, managers who believe that organizations are rational systems often do just that. Even more unfortunately, much of the decisionmaking literature to which managers are exposed implicitly encourages that approach.

Systematic Informality

The 51 percent guide and the use of group settings complement each other. The systematic informality tactic is the third tool in the Savvy's kit to build momentum. Most approaches to influence the organization are either formal and systematic or informal and unsystematic.

When executives feel an issue is vitally important, they generally develop a systematic campaign to address it. Sometimes these issues are management fads that have caught the eye of a senior executive who now wants a program for it in the organization. Example programs that have swept through many companies are Management By Objectives (MBO), strategic planning, quality initiatives, participative management and business process reengineering. Executives and their staffs work hard to organize the materials for the campaign and schedule all the coordinated events and communications necessary to do a systematic quality job. Often the result is a thick, polished, well-indexed notebook that managers take away with them. One executive in a federal agency described such an approach when strategic planning was introduced:

Political Savvy

> *They pulled out all the stops. Each of us filled out extensive planning guides, were assigned to discussion groups, and completed our inputs to the five-year plan. The process was greatly ballyhooed and had all the bells and whistles you could think of. At the end of it we received a glossy, three inch thick report with pictures of executives, logos—the whole bit. There was only one problem: After six months, the reports just sat on the shelf looking pretty but nobody used them for any real decisions.*

This example represents an extreme case of the formal, systematic approach. When used appropriately, it can be an excellent way to *communicate* about issues and a direction people already buy into. But such formal approaches run a high risk of failure when used as the primary means of influence for a new idea or initiative. It's very easy for such an approach to become the ideology of the moment instead of actual practice in the organization.

The major strength of formal approaches is that they tend to be inherently systematic. The major weakness of systematic approaches is that they tend to be overly formal. Genuine human influence occurs more easily through informal channels. Informal approaches allow people to be more themselves, express their true opinions, and not just salute the party line. The major weakness of most informal approaches, however, is that they tend to be haphazard. Managers who use formal methods gain the advantage of being systematic, while informal managers have a higher probability of exercising true influence.

Politically savvy managers try to capture the best of both approaches. They can be seen practicing Management By Walking Around (MBWA) but not just to stay in touch with subordinates, as recommended by many leadership texts. Their use of MBWA expands the traditional approach in two ways. First, they practice it beyond subordinates and include superiors, departmental peers, and people in other departments.

Second, while they use the approach to stay in touch, they also use it to exert influence and learn about other people's agendas. What looks like just shooting the breeze in an unscheduled, casual fashion is used by savvy individuals to do what they call "dripping water on an idea" or "seeding the organization."

Dropping by may appear random and accidental but is actually used strategically by the Savvy as a systematically informal way of working the human system. Informality increases the odds for influence, and their guide to being systematic is generally derived from some form of the Organization Politics Map they have in their heads.

The Machs use this same method, of course. This may be one reason why managers who don't want to be seen as manipulative stick with the more formal methods. The systematic informality approach is another powerful double edged sword. It can be used by Machs to serve their self interests or by the Savvy to serve the organization's interests. A few managers have commented that using systematic informality is obvious. When asked for an example of when they last used this approach, however, many are hard-pressed to answer.

Playing above Board

Some managers find it difficult to view "playing above board" as a tactic. It's as if tactics automatically imply something sneaky. Yet every ethical marketing strategy has tactics. Even "truth in advertising" is a tactic.

Playing above board is one of the most powerful tactics available to the politically Savvy. It is an integral part of being ethical and it has several advantages when building momentum. First, it's easier to develop coalitions if you can be open about what you're trying to do. Second, it generates credibility over time. Since the influence game is tricky and motives are easily suspect, developing a reputation for playing above board greatly enhances the willingness of other executives to listen. It helps create the credibility links (solid lines) seen on the Organization Politics Map. The more such links, the more channels one can travel in navigating the human system.

Political Savvy

Managers often find it difficult to visualize how playing above board works in leadership behind-the-scenes. Take the Chromium Project as an example. The basic strategy calls for Alice to talk with Bill. Playing above board in that situation might have looked like this: Alice drops by Bill's office and says,

> *Hi Bill, have you got a minute? Bill, this meeting on the Chromium Project is coming up on Friday and I think it's a very important decision for the future of the company. Here's how I see the situation. Right now, it doesn't look too good, since Owen and Tom don't seem to see the same merits in the project as I do. It's also clear to me that, without your support, I don't have much hope of convincing the others of the project's benefits.*
>
> *Bill, I truly believe the Chromium Project is vital to the future success of Milford. I know people see this as my idea and are therefore somewhat suspicious. But my understanding of why I was brought into the company was to bring in a fresh perspective and new ideas. So I see it as doing my job.*
>
> *My staff and I have taken a look at the numbers and we believe that if we hold off on the Tensil Strength Project we can meet the cash flow requirements and proceed with a project that I sincerely believe will give us a distinct competitive advantage in the marketplace. Here are some specifics ....*
>
> *I know you were looking to the Tensil Strength Project as a chance to demonstrate the expertise of your department. Well, Bill, as I see it, the new technology for the Chromium Project can be handled inside or outside Milford. I'd be completely willing to recommend that we use our own in-house resources to do the job.*
>
> *Does all this make sense to you? If so, would you be willing to talk to Craig about the Chromium Project? I think he's undecided but would agree to support the project if he understood all the facts. I'd go to him myself but I think you have a much better relationship with him and he would more easily believe you in this particular case. What's your reaction?*

Building Momentum

Alice is being ethical and open with Bill. She's not manipulating him, but she is actively trying to influence him and seek his cooperation. She is playing above board, while following her coalition's strategy. If managers care about their ideas, believe they are beneficial to the company, and try to make winners by satisfying other people's agendas, then playing above board is a viable tactic. Linking agendas in an ethical way is a very powerful approach to building momentum.

The four tactics—the 51 percent guide, use of group settings, systematic informality, and playing above board—are synergistic. Taken together, they create a generic approach for building momentum that can be flexibly modified to fit a variety of situations. For example, start with an exploratory group session. Based upon information from that session, update the political map and potential agenda linkages. Then systematically work the human system. Arrange informal encounters with key managers. Ensure those with at least 51 percent of the influence are favorable to exploring the issue further. Play above board in explaining the idea and in linking agendas. Then, if a critical mass of consensus has begun to build, hold a formal group meeting to close on the decision and make it official. If it hasn't been possible to build momentum for the idea, then it would seem prudent to put off a formal decision meeting. Either the idea doesn't have sufficient merit on its own, or it's less important than other existing agendas, or its time has not yet come. In any case, the savvy manager who still believes in the idea will pull back and wait for the next window of opportunity.

One manager remarked about the tactics for building momentum, "Isn't that just the common sense management adage of 'getting your ducks in a row' before the meeting?" In one sense, yes. However, in practice, using these tactics systematically represents "uncommon sense."

Breaking down the behavior of the intuitively Savvy into its underlying components usually reveals some version of these tactics. As long as the tactics are used intuitively rather than consciously, however, there not only is a greater chance for mishap, but also, a lesser probability that other managers will learn to use them. Therefore, in executing an overall strategy, these tactics should be a more conscious part of every savvy manager's kit bag for taking action.

The Many-Few-Many-Few Technique: Building Momentum in Large Populations

The tactics specified thus far are useful in most situations but are particularly valuable when there are fewer than twenty players. What about building momentum for an entire organization? For groups larger than twenty and up to the thousands, an additional management technique for building momentum has been evolving. It synthesizes decades of experience with employee participation efforts. One way of describing the evolution of the technique is the following:

> *In the beginning, there was the Few-Few approach. That is, a few people (sometimes just one person) at the top of the organization saw themselves as the primary sources of information and as the primary decision makers. Good ideas were thought to come mostly from the top since the top had the most experience and broadest perspective. In stable, less complex times, this process of limiting input to a few and having them decide was not perfect but worked relatively well. For thousands of years it was the best way available to avoid chaos and provide order.*

> *As the pace of change picked up over the eons and the world became more complex, however, decisions went beyond a single person's mind size—the mental capacity to do it all. Post-World War II industry required broader input. Organizations began to recognize that there were good ideas at all levels. In the 1960s, the Many-Many approach emerged. Trying to capitalize on the view that good ideas are widely distributed throughout the organization, participative management and consensus decision making became the rage. Many people were asked for their ideas and many were asked to decide together. While this was great for getting people to buy in, persistent*

snags developed. It took a tremendous amount of time ("We are always in meetings."), the decision-making process slowed ("I used to be able to make this type of a decision in an hour; now, consensus takes three weeks, and the work is suffering."), and managers began to feel they were either giving away power or abdicating their responsibility ("There's no individual accountability anymore; everyone hides behind the committee.").

As the inefficiency, perceived loss of control, and other difficulties of the Many-Many approach surfaced, a lot of management teams went back to the Few-Few approach and participative methods went to the back of the bus. However, the dilemma still remained. In dynamic, complex, changing environments, the Few-Few approach, while good at control, is poor at generating broad-based commitment to action.

Then the Many-Few approach emerged as the possible savior. This technique was designed to capitalize on the fact that good ideas are everywhere but efficient decision making is crucial. The basic approach was to get input from the Many throughout the organization and then let the Few top managers decide. For a while, it seemed like the perfect answer. It maximized employee participation, while maintaining management control and organizational efficiency. Something funny happened on the way to the Many-Few approach, however. Organizations that had been locked into the Few-Few style came out of their dark, smoke-filled rooms. They opened the windows to allow in the fresh views of all types of employees who had ideas relevant to the issue at hand. At first, employees felt great ("Someone is finally asking for my opinion."). Management felt great ("Look at all of these different ideas."). As one might expect, many of the ideas were contradictory since everyone sees things from their own unique perspective. But management sorted through them all, went over various tradeoffs, and came out with the best decision they could, based on all the data. Being action oriented, they then announced and implemented the decision and waited for the kudos to come rolling in from employees who for the first time were given a chance to put their two cents in. Instead, human nature intervened, and all hell broke loose.

Political Savvy

The day after the decision was announced, an employee would knock at the manager's door. "Come in," said the kudos expecting executive. "What the hell is going on here?" demanded the angry employee. "You asked for my opinion and then you went in the opposite direction. What are you trying to pull? If you aren't going to listen to me, then why ask me?" Explanations that there were many contrary opinions tend to fall on deaf ears at this point. The manager, caught off guard by the anger, responded in kind: "Hey! We didn't have to ask for your damn opinion at all. You guys are never satisfied. Now get out of here and get back to work!" The employee slammed the door and the manager slammed the desk. Management then goes back to the Few-Few approach, vowing never again to listen to any guru who advises employee involvement.

This is the point at which a lot of organizations are stuck today. The only problem is that the Few-Few approach still doesn't work well in dynamic environments where problems are complex enough to exceed one manager's mind size. Yet, the Many-Many approach is too inefficient and the Many-Few approach can backfire. What's left? Well, some companies have begun to find ways to build momentum on a large scale. In the politically savvy management of several firms, a technique has started to emerge that offers a way out of some of the inherent dilemmas in building momentum throughout the organization: the *Many-Few-Many-Few* approach. While not an elegant name, it is descriptive of the basic steps involved. These steps are sketched in exhibit 34.

In step one, the issue is sent out to the large numbers of people who may have constructive input or who will be affected by the final decision. If done well, this step breaks the narrowness of the traditional Few-Few approach.

Next, a few key decision makers collect and integrate the diverse input and then make a tentative decision. This step bypasses the major inefficiency of the Many-Many approach. So far, it is the same as the Many-Few approach.

Step three, however, tries to address the human characteristic that often causes the process to backfire if just the first

Building Momentum

two steps are taken. When employees are asked for their opinions, they expect management to act on those opinions. Management gets caught between the "rock" of being expected to act and a "hard place" created by contradictory input. Some contributors, in effect, say go south, others say go north, others say east, and still others say west. Each camp expects its opinions to be acted upon.

What happens next is the critical point in the process of building momentum. Instead of announcing and implementing their decision, the few communicate to the many something like the following: "Thank you for your input regarding the idea we sent out. We received a lot of good suggestions, and, as you might expect, many of them were conflicting." (This is crucial as it's often human nature to believe that our personal opinion reflects that of a much larger audience than it actually does. Unless reminded otherwise, we tend to think the few are ignoring us rather than struggling with diverse ideas. This is when the door slamming occurs.) "We've pulled together your diverse views and added our own knowledge of business direction and resource constraints. It was a tough call but we have come to an initial decision to go northwest and here's why....We'd like to hear your reaction. If this direction still doesn't make sense to you, let us know, and we'll reconsider."

This step three of going out to the many, reminding them that there are vastly different views on the topic, has the effect of diffusing much of the resistance since most people will realize it's a struggle and they still have a second shot at input. The few are no longer seen as making arbitrary decisions that ignore the ideas they sought.

In step four, the few consolidate whatever reactions they receive. These are usually less than one-fifth as many as provoked by the initial request in step one since people often place more value on *having the opportunity* to contribute (such as the right to vote in public elections) than actually *using the opportunity*. The few examine the second round of reactions because sometimes this input raises important questions about the initial decision. The decision is then made final, communicated to

The Many-Few-Many-Few Technique

Step 1: Issue is sent out to the organization for input.

Step 2: Input is synthesized Initial decision is made.

Step 3: Initial decision is communicated and reaction is solicited.

Step 4: Reaction is synthesized. Final decision is made and communicated.

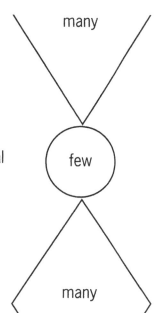
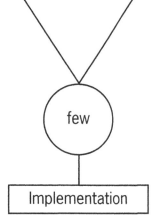

exhibit 34

the many, and then implemented.

The Many-Few-Many-Few is another generic technique and a number of variations exist. While less time-consuming than the Many-Many approach, it still takes enough time that it's best used on issues that have a significant impact on the organization, such as: Should we move corporate headquarters? Should we institute a no-smoking policy? or Should we change our basic ways of operating? When the approach works well, management feels in control throughout the process and employees feel involved and appreciated for their ideas. It's often more important to us that our opinion is valued than necessarily agreed with. While the Many-Few-Many-Few technique has its own set of problems, it does increase the odds for systematically building large-scale momentum in ways that can greatly speed implementation.

SUMMARY OF APPROACHES TO BUILDING MOMENTUM

Much of leadership behind-the-scenes is about building momentum for change. In order to accomplish this, the politically Savvy take risks but they do not operate without a net. The 51 percent guide serves as that net during the high-wire act of implementing strategy. Group settings have their special place in building momentum but require much conscious thought as to their timing and purpose. One doesn't have to be formal to be systematic, and systematic informality is a way of building momentum that fits well with the actual dynamics that influence human systems. Playing above board is not only desirable from an ethical standpoint, but is actually more effective in the long run. With the Many-Few-Many-Few approach, a savvy manager has a template to build momentum on a large scale throughout the organization.

Each of these techniques can add value on its own and are also complimentary. Naturally savvy individuals tend to use one or more of these techniques unconsciously. Few use the full range of techniques consciously. Those that do, however, often become aware that taken together these techniques, and the ones that follow have the potential synergy to greatly increase the success probabilities for an influence attempt.

Chapter 10

CUSTOMIZING ATTEMPTS AT INFLUENCE

All too many administrators use the same tactics repeatedly, regardless of the circumstances.

—Richard H. Buskirk, ... *The Fait Accompli*

Throughout the book we have been taking the implicit process of the intuitively Savvy and making explicit and systematic some of its underlying components. We are now at the point where one has decided to be an active, ethical player, developed a coalition, mapped the political terrain, planned a basic strategy, acquired a decent feel for the cultural ground rules, put together a tool kit of techniques for building momentum, and is now ready to go on line, one-on-one with other managers.

The tactics and techniques described in this chapter go down to the next level of detail in implementing strategy. Whether this level comes across as nit-picking or as the nitty-gritty of day-to-day politics will depend upon your previous organizational experience and your attention to details. Customizing influence will be described in terms of five components: (1) executive attention viewed as a strategic resource, (2) idiosyncrasy management, (3) involvement levels, (4) the mix of planning and acting, and (5) interpersonal diplomacy.

CUSTOMIZING INFLUENCE

Executive Attention as a Strategic Resource

To the rational manager, the words strategic resources conjure up things such as capital, equipment, labor, and the like. For the politically Savvy, however, there is another strategic resource that is considered very tangible, although it is intangible to most people. The Savvy are more likely to view executive attention as described in exhibit 35.

> **Executive Attention**
>
> When it comes to initiating organizational change, the scarcest and most critical of all organizational resources is executive attention.

exhibit 35

Any new idea must have executive attention to survive. It is to a new idea what rain is to a seedling. Without sufficient time devoted to the idea by those in charge, no initiative for change can grow. Failure to view executive attention as a concrete strategic resource can have severe consequences. It causes individuals, who otherwise manage traditional strategic resources extremely well, to mismanage the basic feedstock of most change initiatives.

Far too many managers approach executive meetings and mistake the clean, quiet orderliness of executive offices for calm,

Customizing Attempts at Influence

reasonable environments. In actuality, despite their composed appearances, many executives' lives resemble that poignantly described by a mayor in exhibit 36.

An Aspect of Executive Attention

Being a mayor is like walking on a moving belt while juggling. Right off you have to walk fast enough to stay even. After you have been in the office a short time, people start throwing wads of paper at you, so now you've got to walk, juggle, and duck too. Then the belt starts to move faster and people start throwing wooden blocks at you. About the time you are running like mad, juggling, and ducking stones, someone sets one end of the belt on fire. Now, if you keep the things you are juggling in the air, stay on the belt, put out the fire, and not get seriously injured, you've found the secret to this job. You have managed to put it all together into something that works.

—J. P. Kotter & P. Lawrence, *Mayors in Action*

exhibit 36

A harried individual on a burning treadmill is likely to be a better starting assumption when entering the office of an unknown executive. Taking this view seriously can radically change one's approach. Executives expect their time to be used well. Politeness may restrain them from indicating when it is being abused—but they do remember!

One consequence of executive attention being a scarce resource is the "colliding colleagues" syndrome. For example, any staff function generally consists of several specialists who share the common values of the function. Theoretically, they should represent natural allies in influencing the organization. All too frequently, however, what happens is as described by a human resource executive in an oil company:

> *Here we were as a department, all sharing the same basic values. We believe people are assets to be invested in rather than costs to be reduced. We had a lot of talented individuals and therefore represented a potentially formidable force in moving the company forward. Yet in practice, something entirely different happened. Each specialist operating out of his or her own particular box would generate one or more new programs. We had change initiatives in EEO, compensation, education, succession planning, health care, flexible working hours, high-potential development, career planning, employee involvement, and so forth. At first it seemed great, as we were hitting the executives from all sides. However, knowing that each initiative required top management time and understanding to generate commitment, every specialist developed plans for sitting down with executives to explore the merits of their particular program. Because the vice president of Human Resources encouraged such initiatives, there were several of these sessions, each lasting two or more hours. Since the programs were new, the time allotted was based upon what the professionals thought the program needed in order to be understood.*
>
> *Instead of forming an alliance to change the organization, we ended up overloading and irritating the executives who felt "all this stuff is taking up too much time." We were actually competing against one another to get our particular ideas heard. The potential alliance broke down into a squabbling bunch of professionals, all vying with each other for the attention of top management.*

The politically Savvy view executive attention as a critical, scarce resource. Rather than setting the length of the meeting based upon what the program needs, they base it on what the executive needs. Communications about a new idea are formulated according to what the executives can easily and quickly digest. This means that when using systematic informality, one would also use communication methods that are concise and require minimal time to process the information.

Many professionals try to impress executives with their particular expertise by peppering their conversations with the jargon of their specialty. The Savvy go in the opposite direction.

One savvy manager in the broadcasting industry is known for responding to ideas from his professional staff with, "I think the concept is great. It looks like it will work. Now strip the specialist jargon out and put it into 'execu-speak' (his word for the everyday jargon of the executives)."

Viewing executive attention as a scarce strategic resource magnifies the importance of the next issue in customizing influence.

Managing Idiosyncrasies

The basic principle behind managing idiosyncrasies is that everyone is different. While this is not an earth-shaking insight, it is surprising how many strategies ignore this basic fact of human nature. Managing idiosyncrasies includes considering: (a) how the individual processes information, (b) timing, and (c) individual requirements for validity.

Individual styles of processing. There is substantial evidence that different executives can have vastly different ways of processing information. Some think aloud, and find conversational approaches very effective. Others need to be alone and often prefer written reports over personal conversations.

A second distinction is understanding what kind of information makes an impression. Some executives need to start with the underlying concept before they are ready to get into the details. 'What's the basic idea here?', is the hallmark of the executive who processes information at the conceptual level first. Other executives need concrete details before they can build to the conceptual level. 'Give me the facts and let's see the numbers' are indicators of this style.

Some executives come from the Missouri "show me" school of information processing. They don't want to read any reports or hear a conceptual briefing. They need, somehow, to see, feel, and touch the idea. These executives basically process information using their own experience. Demonstrations, working models, or visits to other organizations where the idea is in use are effective ways of communicating to these executives.

The more one knows about the preferred style of a given executive, the more customized and targeted the approach can be. As a result, the executive's time and attention can be used more efficiently and effectively. Differences in processing styles are yet another reason why information that is presented for the first time in a group setting often ends up more misunderstood than clarified.

The 51 percent guide and systematic informality can make customization easier. They allow different styles to be taken into account individually, rather than having them clash in a group meeting. Circumstances may force a premature presentation, but a savvy manager at least makes sure that the presentation has something for each style, such as alternating between concrete and big-picture images with some simple demonstrations worked in. Some dialogue would be encouraged for those who think out loud, while decisions would be put off, allowing time for those who need solitude to come to their own understanding of the idea.

The major trap most managers fall into is that they assume that their own way of processing information is also the way of others. If they like to absorb facts and details in isolation, they may start by blanketing all the executives with thick reports, and thus unknowingly risk sabotaging their influence attempt. Managers who fall into this trap can be heard saying things like: "I don't know why support for this idea isn't developing The head of finance liked it and it is such a good report."

Savvy managers learn as much as possible about how key executives process information. They might then develop a detailed report for some, a conceptual white paper for others, and a site visit for still others, all within a systematically informal approach.

Timing. Executives differ as to the parts of the day in which they are most productive or most receptive to new ideas. For certain aspects of implementing strategy, the adage timing

Customizing Attempts at Influence

is everything holds true. An ill-timed attempt is often worse than no attempt at all.

One way of looking at managers is as devices for processing information for the organization. They take in data, sort it, assign it to categories, match it against their experience and goals, and come out with a decision. That is why knowing how they process information is important. The issue of timing also relates to processing information and has interesting analogies to a computer. This issue concerns knowing what shape an individual's central processing unit is in. Some executives' mental computers aren't even up and running until after two cups of coffee in the morning. Dropping by early may impress them with one's eagerness, but don't count on their understanding the information.

Indicators that the executive computer is working effectively are high energy, relaxed attitude, and good mood. Many executives have patterns during the day and the week based on regular events and their own body clocks. These patterns can indicate periods with a high or low probability of their being influenced.

Bad moods have the effect of short circuiting an executive's central processing unit. That's one reason why many sales representatives routinely become friendly with the executive's secretary. They can ask how the boss is feeling today and get a quick reading on whether the customer's mental computer is up and ready for input. Savvy managers notice various executive patterns and take constant readings of mood and readiness. They often start the conversation with "Is this a good time to discuss...?" This simple question not only gives them a direct answer on the timing issue but also indicates respect for the executive's total situation.

Another issue related to timing is overload. When a computer becomes overloaded with information, it shuts down. A similar thing happens to humans. Approaching an executive just prior to an important meeting, during a crisis, or at the end of a long, hard day generally demonstrates a poor understanding of timing.

Political Savvy

Systematic informality gives a manager maximum flexibility in choosing the appropriate time to exert influence. The best times for an executive to process new information may be over a relaxed lunch, during a meeting break, over a drink after work, right after a vacation, at mid-morning, or after the budget review. While it may seem manipulative to some, other intuitive managers view it as common sense and have been doing it without thinking their entire careers. The Savvy know that choosing the right timing respects the unique characteristics of each individual and maximizes the probability of having influence.

Individual requirements for validity. Executives can differ widely on what they need in order to consider a new idea valid. Those with scientific, engineering, and analytical backgrounds are often data hounds and require scientific and statistical proof of a new concept. "Let's look at the statistics" or "What's the research on the issue?" are questions asked by such executives. As one savvy manager reported, "I know that the vice president of Marketing is going to ask right away, 'What are the numbers?'. That's the only thing that seems to count with him, so that's the part I focus on in our discussions."

A significant number of executives, on the other hand, rely more on anecdotal evidence. While the data hound wants the numbers, these executives may be more impressed with a meaningful example or story. For example, a manager in the appliance industry remarked about a new initiative to increase product quality, "We got Jim on board with the quality initiative after we told him my wife bought one of our toasters and received a painful electric shock when she plugged it in." Other executives are less impressed with data and anecdotes than with what competitors are doing. One manager in a porcelain manufacturing firm told the following story:

> *We tried everything to convince our vice president to move to a higher level computerized inventory system. We had research showing reliable numbers on cost savings, we showed him that other executives supported it, we even gave him a mock demon-*

stration. But nothing worked until he found out that our chief competitor was building such a system. Then all of a sudden he went from opposing the idea to being its champion. It was amazing what a difference it made to hear that Company X might be moving ahead of us.

Then there are the executives who value personal credibility more than any other factor. They know one can lie with statistics, and they don't go by simple anecdotes or really care what the competition is doing. These executives tend to believe that the world is very complex and therefore what makes an idea valid for them is to hear it from someone they trust. A manager in the IRS gave the following account:

I had been trying for months to get the department head to switch paper suppliers. I had the cost facts and figures. The data seemed overwhelming in favor of the change. But nothing happened until I expressed my exasperation to a manager in another department. Well, it turned out that he was a long time friend of my department head and they played golf every month. The idea made sense to him and he said he would do what he could. The very next Monday my department head dropped by my office and said he had been thinking more about the idea over the weekend and had concluded that we should change paper suppliers. I felt simultaneously blown away, very pleased, and frustrated at the way the system seemed to work.

Many such executives in a changing world full of ideas come to rely more on respected colleagues than on reports. This is one of the reasons why Alice's strategy called for following the credibility links in the Chromium Project case rather than presenting all the objective facts to everyone herself.

The different types of validity have been associated thus far with individual managers. In practice, such pure types are in the minority. Most managers use various combinations of these types to make their judgments on the merit of an idea.

While many of these requirements are specific to a particular executive, there is one type of validity that seems to work with almost everyone. It's called convergent validity and was discussed in another light when we addressed the value of coalitions in chapter six. If one hears the same remark from several different people, it tends to have much more credibility than a long lecture from a single person.

Convergent validity from multiple sources is one of the most powerful means of influence. An employee may write off a three-hour feedback session about his arrogance from the boss by labeling the whole thing as a personality conflict: Larry just doesn't like the fact that I'm confident and he's not. It is extremely difficult, however, for the same person to ignore comments about coming across as arrogant from several different people within a period of a few weeks. To verify that convergent validity has such a strong influence, just have three separate people tell someone in the same day, "You really look tired", and see if that person doesn't seriously begin to examine the truth of the assertion. Generally, the more an executive hears the same information from several different sources, the more valid the information will seem.

Involvement: A Double-Edged Sword

A third way to customize influence is the tactical use of involvement. Exhibit 37 illustrates seven levels, each implying a different degree of interaction and sense of ownership in the change initiative. Most managers are familiar with these levels but usually do not consciously consider them in relation to each other or as a part of a systematic influence approach.

No information. This is the level of zero inclusion. It has tactical value in that it may be premature to involve some people until the idea has reached a certain stage of development. "Let's not bother Jim with this right now. He's got enough on his plate and we don't even know if we fully believe in the idea yet," commented one executive in an example of this level.

The Machs can also use this tactic, of course, to deliberately keep certain managers from knowing about a project until it's too late. Each tactic can be used for good or ill, depending

Customizing Attempts at Influence

Levels of Involvement

Involvement		Interaction	Ownership
Very Low	1. No Information	None	None
	2 Placed on Distribution Lists		
	A. Information Only	None	Low
	B. Feedback /Recommendations Requested	Low	Low to Moderate
	3. Special Reports Tailored to Individuals		
	A. Information Only	None	None to Low
	B. Feedback /Recommendations Requested	Low to Moderate	Low to Moderate
	4. Oral Presentations		
	A. Formal	Moderate	Low to Moderate
	B. Informal	Moderate to High	Moderate to High
	5. Observer	Low to Moderate	Moderate
	6. Consultant	High	High
Very High	7 Participant	Very High	Very High

exhibit 37

on the ethics and intent of the user.

Distribution lists. This level represents the least involvement when customizing influence. There are a couple of sublevels. The first is FYI (For Your Information). It is a one way, written message and is used to let specified individuals know that something is going on. Its form can range from the standard memo to entire reports or white papers. There is no interaction because it is a one-way communication. It can create a small amount of ownership since the recipients feel they are at least important enough to be kept informed.

The second sublevel is basically the same as the first, with one important exception. Instead of being stamped "FYI," it is stamped something like "FYI and reactions requested." This addition allows for some minimal two-way dialogue. Interaction is initiated or at least permitted. Ownership increases the more individuals believe they can put their two cents in. It's a mild way to initiate the Many-Few-Many-Few approach.

Special reports. This level is tailored to specific individuals, with different information-processing styles taken into account. One executive may receive a two-page summary while another is sent a report rich in data with supporting computer printouts. The point is that too often managers assume everyone should be involved in the same way, so they send the same type of report to everyone, regardless of different preferences in processing information. Such customization can occur without creating equity problems by sending a special cover note to each executive. Again, while some may view such differentiation as potentially manipulative, the Savvy recognize it as trying to manage each executive's time well.

As with distribution lists, special reports can be FYI, or they can ask for comments. The more that interaction and customization are designed into an involvement approach, the more likely a sense of ownership will build.

Oral presentations. When used well, the spoken word has distinct advantages over the written word. Written communications suffer from being read out of context. Clarifying questions and face-to-face dialogue are virtually absent. Oral communications allow for intonations and hundreds of other cues that imply how seriously the information is to be taken and what interpretations are to be made. During oral presentations both parties, the sender and the receiver, are present at the same time and place. For these and other reasons easily obtained from any text on communications, oral presentations are a much richer communication vehicle.

Such presentations can be formal or informal. It is very popular in some organizations to make formal presentations with overhead projectors and stacks of view foils. The advan-

Customizing Attempts at Influence

tages of the formal presentation are that it is live, the key players are in the room, and the visuals are often more easily absorbed than thick reports. Since most formal presentations end in a question and-answer period, this format also allows for a measure of interaction.

Unfortunately, the formal oral presentation can have severe disadvantages as means of influence. It can become a "dog and pony show" when it's delivered repeatedly in the same way to several audiences. Such presentations are often the prime vehicle for some managers' attempts to influence the organization. The risk of relying too much on this method is that it can bypass the 51 percent guide, systematic informality, and the appropriate use of small group settings for building momentum. Often cultural norms subtly build around dog and pony shows. People learn to ask only polite questions and not state their true opinions. If a formal oral presentation is used at the beginning or end of the process of influencing the organization, however, it can be a valuable part of an effective approach. This is particularly true when systematic informality and the 51 percent guide have been used prior to the presentation. After the decision is made, an oral presentation can be an excellent vehicle to communicate (rather than influence) that decision.

In informal oral presentations, the few slides that may be used are customized to the information-processing styles of key managers. This format better fits the systematically informal approach. It involves individuals or small groups, in which the presentation is designed less as the centerpiece and more as the stimulus to a candid dialogue. It is this candid dialogue that then becomes the major focus of the session.

Because of their potential for live interaction, both forms of oral presentations can increase a sense of ownership if run effectively. Again, they are best thought of as supporting parts and not as the main vehicle for influence.

Observer. Seeing something in action creates a deeper level of understanding, particularly for the "Show me, I'm from Missouri" type of executive. Seeing conveys a great deal more information than reading or hearing. Observing can include having an executive watch a quality circle in action or a demonstration of a new global communications system, or visiting an organization where a new idea is already working.

A potential disadvantage of observing is that it often takes more of an executive's time than a memo or short presentation. A general rule of thumb among the Savvy is that the more time the executive puts into something, the more value the executive expects to get out of it.

Consultant. This next level is the first one in which the executive gets personally involved. In essence, the executive is asked to be an advisor in some fashion. One can be invited in at this level with words such as: Jack, we have an idea for a new billing system. We know you have some background in this area and we'd really appreciate your taking a look at the idea and giving us your advice.

This approach is particularly valuable with executives who show initial interest in an idea. It's also useful with those who are not against the idea and are willing to explore it further. It does require more time than previous levels of interaction. If it works, however, it can generate a tremendous sense of ownership, since the executive's own views have been incorporated. Additionally, instead of being treated as an outsider, as at previous levels, this approach invites the manager in. It demonstrates that the executive is valued and has something to contribute for which credit can be given later.

Participant. This level represents the deepest involvement because the executive is invited to participate directly. It differs from the consultant level in that the executive inherently feels a part of the process and has a piece of the action. It is particularly useful with those who have the hear-see-touch style of processing information.

Everyone in the strategy coalition is at the participant level, as is each person who is actively advocating further exploration of the idea. An executive who has been asked to be a sponsor of the project is included at this level.

The participant level has the potential for creating the most

Customizing Attempts at Influence

ownership in a change initiative. It is very difficult to participate in a good initiative without developing some commitment to the project. How this level is used depends upon the particular nature of the change being proposed and the unique characteristics of the executive.

The Downsides of Inclusion

Thus far it might be easy to conclude that the deeper the involvement level, the better. Not necessarily! Machs who are against, or feel somehow threatened by a project often maneuver to be included. It is a prime way to gather "ammunition" useful in shooting down the proposal later. Sometimes this type of maneuvering is hard to spot until after the fact, and then it's too late. One manager in an aerospace company described such a case:

> *It turned out that our prime mistake was getting Paul, the vice president of Manufacturing, involved too early in the process. While he never did express great enthusiasm for the Zadon Project, he did seem interested and said he'd like to play an active role in its development. At first we were thrilled. With this vice president's backing, the project would have a real chance. We invited Paul to several of our internal planning meetings. He asked many questions and even gave several helpful suggestions. We thought we were really on a roll. Then the bomb dropped.*
>
> *I was called into the CEO's office and was told that the executive committee had decided to divert the funds from the Zadon Project to another one. He apologized but told me that it was in the best interest of the company. Our group was split apart and assigned to other projects.*
>
> *We found out later that Paul had argued convincingly* **against** *the project. Every new idea has its flaws and risks. It seemed that Paul had used his involvement and knowledge of the project's inner workings to build an impressive case against it by connecting every possible flaw and risk. From what we heard, he was very smooth in the executive committee meeting. He*

was quoted as saying, "Gentlemen, I had high hopes for the Zadon Project and even got involved myself. However, I feel it's my duty to tell you that we may be wasting the shareholders' money." He then described in authoritative detail the potential problems associated with continuing the project. The project funds were then diverted to one of his own ideas.

The level of inclusion offered to each person can be an aspect of carrying out strategy. The more exposure key managers have to the idea, the more they can either back it or undermine it, depending upon their purpose. That's why inclusion is a double-edged sword and is best planned with full awareness of the risks.

PLAN-ACT MATRIX

Most of us know people who meticulously plan everything down to the finest detail. At the extreme, such planning extends to parties, picnics, and other events that are inherently spontaneous. It seems to them that if they don't have everything planned out exactly, something will go terribly wrong. On the other hand, there are those who seem to avoid planning like the plague. They often seem to be shooting from the hip and prefer to play it by ear. Either approach can be very beneficial or extremely dangerous.

Managers have a choice when-implementing a strategy as to how much to *plan* ahead of time versus how much to *act* and see what happens. This choice should depend more upon the environment in which they are operating than on their personal style.

Two key assumptions about the political environment and how they might guide the mix of planning and acting in customizing one's strategy are displayed in exhibit 38. The first has to do with how much candid feedback there is, and the second deals with the price of the mistake. Each of these assumptions represents an important dimension to consider when implementing any strategy. Taken together, the amount of feedback

Customizing Attempts at Influence

in the environment and the cost of making an error determine which mix of planning and acting is likely to be most effective. Most managers can readily identify these two dimensions in their own organizations.

Plan-Act Matrix

Environment is:

	Environment is feedback:	
	Poor	**Rich**
Benevolent	Act or Plan First — Your Choice	**ACT** — Then Adjust
Malevolent	**PLAN** Completely	**PLAN** next step, **ACT, PLAN,** etc…

exhibit 38

Environmental Feedback

Each action by a manager produces a reaction in others. The first question to raise about a particular organization's environment is whether it is feedback rich or poor. If the organization is feedback rich, others will readily express their opinions of a new idea. This means a great deal of new information about the political terrain will be learned at each stage of action.

If the environment is feedback poor, it means one may not find out for weeks or maybe never how a presentation or discussion was actually received. It is sometimes the norm in polite cultures to praise every presentation; in that case, the environment may look feedback rich but may really be quite feedback poor.

Political Savvy

The second indicator relevant to customizing the mix of planning and acting is whether the environment treats mistakes benevolently or malevolently, that is, whether the cost of a mistake is low or high. A mistake in a benevolent environment costs very little. As a finance manager in a canning company described her environment, "This place is full of second chances. What counts is your long run batting average."

In a malevolent environment, one false step can be disastrous. "Around here you really have to watch your p's and q's. There's almost no tolerance for being wrong. One mistake and you could be history," is how a manager in a fast-food company described the executive suite.

Plotting these two dimensions allows implementation to be customized in one of four basic ways, as illustrated in the Plan-Act Matrix.

> **When to plan every step:**
> **The feedback poor, malevolent environment**

The bottom left square of the matrix characterizes an environment in which: (1) a manager may never learn the truth about how a proposal was truly received, and (2) a mistake can kill the project. A long time may pass before the manager even learns that a mistake was made. How many managers are walking around today thinking everything is okay when most other people know that the individual has been quietly "written off?"

In feedback poor, malevolent organizations, the best way to customize implementation is to plan extensively. Create an overall approach; then plan every detail conservatively. Develop some form of the Organization Politics Map with great care and validate it as much as possible beforehand, create an extensive intelligence network to collect a maximum amount of information, and ask a lot of discreet questions during the process of building momentum. Managers who become Cynics often got that way after being burned by this type of environment. "Hip shooters" and spontaneous individuals tend not to last long in these types of organizations.

> **When to play it by ear:**
> **The feedback rich, benevolent environment**

The upper right square in the matrix represents feedback rich, benevolent conditions. It requires a mix of planning and acting opposite to the preceding one. When the environment is feedback rich, a manager will quickly learn the candid reactions of others. In a benevolent environment, the price of a misstep is likely to be small. Once a basic strategy has been developed, playing it by ear in carrying out the strategy is not only permissible but can be even more effective than planning every detail extensively.

Most situations are more complex and dynamic than any detailed plan can account for. Once a general strategy has been developed, just acting will produce a constant stream of valuable information. Feedback rich, benevolent environments allow strategy implementation to be flexible and self-adjusting.

Too much planning can actually be detrimental in this environment. The risk is that through the laborious process of creating the plan, managers may become wedded to it. Even when new information calls for a change in the plan, it can take on a life of its own and be followed blindly.

Most organizations would like to create feedback rich, benevolent environments. It is the best environment for learning and constructive risk taking, so vital in an age of global competition. This is the kind of environment that allows children to have fun while they develop skills. It's an environment in which mistakes are not harmful but actually beneficial to the learning process.

Most managers would not characterize their organizations

as being feedback rich and benevolent, but there are pockets in which these two environmental conditions are found in many companies. "Skunk works" operations and brainstorming sessions deliberately try to create this environment. High performance, high energy teams often create this feedback rich, benevolent environment for themselves. These conditions can also exist between two individuals. A prime example are people who are connected by credibility links, with the result that discussions go smoother and are much more effective. It's another reason why following credibility paths is stressed so much in politically savvy strategy.

> **When to plan one small step at a time:**
> **The feedback rich, malevolent environment**

What about environments that are feedback rich but malevolent? A manager will receive a great deal of feedback instantly, but a misstep could be deadly. In this environment, the Plan-Act Matrix calls for an overall approach that is carried out in planned, small, half-steps.

In the context of being politically savvy, a half-step is an action that is low profile and open ended. Carefully planned half steps are appropriate for two reasons. First, each step will provide a great deal of useful information. Second, taking one half-step at a time minimizes the negative impact of a mistake. A major presentation to an unknown audience when an official decision is to be made risks disaster in this environment. Instead, one should carefully follow the tactics for building organizational momentum. Using the 51 percent guide informally is particularly fitting in this type of environment.

A half-step is characterized by its "fail-functional" design. While each action is designed to succeed, each action is also designed so that should something go wrong all is not lost. A

Customizing Attempts at Influence

good example of such a design is an escalator which is deliberately constructed so that if it fails, it becomes a stairway and remains functional. If, instead, a failed escalator became a slide, then it would be impassable and there would be few escalators in buildings today.

For new ideas, a formal presentation given at a group meeting in which a decision will be made represents too large of a step because it lacks a fail-functional design. If something goes wrong there may be no second chances. Setting up an informal chat with a key executive, on the other hand, is a small step with a fail-functional aspect designed in. The idea may fail to be communicated, but since it was an informal setting, no final decision was made and there is still an opportunity to come back to that executive. Also, one may have obtained valuable information about possible objections to the idea which can be strategized and incorporated into future communications. Even at a meeting where an official decision will be made, tabling an idea that's in trouble represents a half-step that can be taken on the spot. It removes the idea from discussion before a premature decision can be made against it, and thus allows more time to develop a better communication approach.

**When to use your natural style:
The feedback poor, benevolent environment**

The fourth square in the Plan-Act Matrix indicates environments that are feedback poor but benevolent, that is, one in which there may not be much feedback, but a mistake is not costly. In this environment a general plan is called for, but there are no strong guidelines emphasizing planning or acting. Here a manager's own personal style is a viable guide.

PLAN-ACT MATRIX SUMMARY

As throughout the book, the basic point of this section is to raise assumptions and make conscious decisions, this time about the right mix of planning and acting. The Plan-Act Matrix can help individuals who have developed either a strong planning or strong acting bias to reexamine their assumptions. A particular bias may be quite useful in an environment with one type of feedback but harmful in another. Politically savvy managers work to find the right mix of planning and acting when customizing their attempts at influence. This customization can occur at two levels, one for the situation as a whole, and the other when gauging how to approach a specific individual.

INTERPERSONAL DIPLOMACY

Next we come to interpersonal diplomacy. Many people who would pick up a book entitled *Political Savvy* might expect it to be full of tips on interpersonal skills useful in political situations. A strong message in this book is that while interpersonal skill is certainly helpful in working the human system, it is by no means the key to becoming politically savvy. In fact, the interpersonally skillful can be so blessed with charisma that they too often rest on their charms and fail to develop and use the range of strategic tools necessary to become truly savvy. Interpersonal skill has deliberately not been mentioned until this chapter, and then only as one of several customizing techniques. There are plenty of books that deal with various interpersonal skills used to gain power. Some are listed in the Further Readings section in the back of this book.

The focus here is on interpersonal diplomacy, which means influencing the organization in ways that minimize the creation of losers. Four basic tactics in interpersonal diplomacy are spread the credit, foster face-saving, use the "two shots-then-salute" technique, and adopt a long-term view.

Customizing Attempts at Influence

> **Spread the credit.**

People who truly work for the good of the whole organization do this. They realize that the greater number of people who receive credit for a new idea, the more powerful the organization begins to feel. The Savvy are therefore skilled at giving credit. They seek out opportunities to make others winners while generally avoiding a high profile for themselves. As emphasized earlier, being savvy requires a relatively healthy ego that takes more satisfaction in making something work than in gaining status.

Of course, this tactic drives the Machs a little crazy. In their opinion, taking credit and not giving it away is the whole name of the game. With their win-lose view of organizational life, they assume that since someone has to win, it might as well be them. How can you get promoted unless you are seen as the one who deserves the credit for something?

Now, the Savvy aren't stupid about their careers. They are in the game for a different purpose, that is, to make a contribution and achieve a win-win outcome. They are not overly humble, an attitude that often backfires, and they do enjoy the advancement that brings increased responsibility and raises the standard of living for their families. But a funny thing often happens on the way to giving credit: it comes back multiplied. An executive in a timber company remarked, "Our CEO got to that position by constantly giving credit to everyone else. He created so much good will in the system that he had many people wanting to make him a success. They did and he was."

Next time a person who is considered a real leader speaks at the end of a successful project, watch how much credit is given to a wide variety of people. It is hard to praise others without receiving credit in return. Tailoring credit to individual preferences—public recognition or a private pat on the back, tangible short-term bonuses or intangible long-term opportunities—maximizes the impact of giving credit.

Foster face-saving

While the Savvy strive for the win-win solutions among multiple agendas, organizational realities all too often dictate that some individuals lose or at least feel they have lost. The Machs may take some glee in triumphing over others, but the Savvy do not or are less inclined to do so. The Machs often view organizational life as a competition and so creating losers adds joy to the victory, whereas the Savvy view losers as unfortunate outcomes of scarce resources or results of the impossibility of finding win-win solutions. They seem to see the wisdom in Katherine Hepburn's dictum, "In a long-term relationship, any time you win, you lose." If their project is chosen over another's, they are gracious winners and even give credit to the losing project for its merits. Whether in marriages or organizations, triumphing in arguments or issues is risky business, for it often creates a desire to get back at the victor rather than fostering greater cooperation and rational problem solving.

On-the-Spot Face-Saving

> A man walks into a grocery store. He goes up to the boy stocking the vegetables and asks for a half a head of lettuce. The stock boy replies, "I don't know. I'll have to ask the manager." As he goes through the doors to the receiving dock where the manager is, he doesn't know that the customer is following right behind him. He calls out to the manager, "Hey, Jack, some jerk out here wants to buy a half a head of lettuce." From the manager's facial expression, he can tell something's up and immediately notices the customer standing behind him. Without skipping a beat, he says, "and this gracious gentleman has kindly agreed to take the other half off our hands."

exhibit 39

There are other tactics that foster face-saving. These include praising the fine effort put in by the people associated with a losing project, welcoming those who lost to join in making the accepted project a success, and employing good interpersonal skills (see, for example, exhibit 39). There are times when nothing helps, but savvy individuals work hard at minimizing the experience of losing for others.

The Two-Shots-Then-Salute Technique

If fostering face-saving is a way of gracious winning, then the technique summarized in exhibit 40 represents an aspect of gracious losing. It is a specific form of intelligent risk taking that can be quite valuable when attempting to influence the organization. It allows you either to take a risk and be successful or to use the loss to demonstrate that you are a team player.

The Two-Shots-Then-Salute Technique

In attempting to influence an individual or group about a new or controversial idea:

1) **Take a shot at it.** Explain the idea and its potential benefits. If this idea is accepted, fine. If not,

2) **Take a second shot at it.** Learn from the first attempt and customize further, based upon the particular audience. If it is accepted, fine. If not,

3) **Salute.** Make a sincere commitment to implement whatever the organization has decided to do.

---

exhibit 40

This technique is deceptively simple. It looks easy but is actually relatively rare in organizational life. First, many individuals never take a shot at presenting a new idea. In organizations that avoid taking risks, presenting a new or controversial idea brings on ridicule and fault finding more often than praise. In such organizations, managers have learned the hard way that presenting an idea that disturbs the status quo is not a smart career move. As a result, these organizations tend to churn out the classic yes-men who still plague large parts of corporate America. They become full of people who seldom, if ever, take a shot at a new idea but rather salute anything suggested by those in power. In such organizations, saluting has long been a primary mechanism for preserving one's job.

While an organization may be populated mostly by saluters, there are generally some individuals who constantly take shots at trying to change the system. These shooters can help an organization progress by questioning the status quo, but, unfortunately, some of them never stop shooting. Their persistent dissatisfaction with the status quo can lead them to overload the system with new ideas.

Another nasty habit tends to creep into persistent shooters. They become so attached to and invested in their ideas that, if the organization chooses a different direction, they become upset and refuse to salute. Thus, they become ungracious losers and often feel it would compromise their integrity to make a commitment to any course of action but the one they believe in. Eventually, they quit of their own accord or are forced out by the organization. This only reinforces the saluters who want to safeguard their own jobs. Like the pike fish, they learn once again that they can't get the guppies. Taking a shot at a new idea is confirmed as a dangerous thing to do and saluting remains the golden path to security.

After hearing the above, one executive remarked, "You've just hit the nail on the head in describing what I'm experiencing in my company. I've got plenty of saluters who are afraid to bring forth new ideas, and I've got a minority of shooters who have some decent ideas but who refuse to join the team if their ideas aren't chosen. What I need are people who know how to do both."

The two-shots-then-salute technique represents a generic form of such a combination. In practice, there are multiple variations of it that can be customized to a given situation. The technique is based on previously discussed assumptions about how human nature operates in organizations. First, it builds off the assumption that new and controversial ideas are difficult to comprehend upon initial hearing. That's why taking the first shot often doesn't work but is still very useful because it helps one customize the second shot.

Another assumption is that organizations are loaded with people vying for scarce executive attention. Everyone wants more time to press their personal opinions upon executives who may feel overloaded already, such as the mayor on the treadmill in exhibit 36. In practice, this means that after a few shots one risks being perceived as abusing executive time.

Third, helping an organization implement a decision opposite to one's own proposal does not imply a lack of personal or professional integrity. On the contrary, it can represent a higher form of integrity. In one sense, the executive level is a marketplace of ideas, all of which cannot be implemented. Once people have had a fair opportunity to market their ideas by taking their two shots, teamwork becomes paramount. Putting personal opinions aside and saluting by sincerely working for what the organization has decided upon demonstrates this sense of teamwork in a powerful way. It shows a willingness to subordinate personal preferences to the overriding decision of the company. Such teamwork is absolutely essential if the organization is to survive over the long term.

The fourth assumption about human nature in organizations is that if executives know a manager will eventually commit to what the organization decides, there is a natural tendency to really listen to that manager's ideas. If they believe a manager is not ever likely to salute, however, they tend to shut down the idea prematurely so that a troublemaker isn't created.

In some parts of an organization where the two-shots then salute technique becomes an operational norm, even long-standing saluters start to feel safe enough to offer a different idea, realizing it won't be taken as a sign of disloyalty.

Of course, if the direction the organization chooses violates deeply held personal values, that person should take the proper action. It may mean leaving the organization or blowing the whistle on an illegal act. Apart from such an extreme situation, the two-shots-then-salute technique increases a manager's ability to safely take a shot at influencing the organization.

> Adopt a Long-Term Orientation.

Spreading credit, fostering face-saving, and two-shots then salute all work best if a manager adopts a long-term perspective. The importance of a long-term perspective cannot be overstated. It can make the difference between a career of major contributions to one characterized by early burnout.

Savvy managers typically seem to have a longer view than other managers. They are able to make the critical distinction between individual battles and the overall war. They seem to understand instinctively that if you see every issue as a life or death situation, then you will die many times. It is one of the reasons why they can lose gracefully. Knowing that the organization pendulum is constantly swinging, they await another time when their ideas may become acceptable.

A long-term view also makes spreading credit not just a nice thing to do but also smart. A chit is created in the system every time credit is given. The Savvy may sacrifice personal glory in the short run, but they can build a tremendous store of influence chits in the long run. These can be cashed in at some decisive point in the future.

Fostering face-saving also makes sense from a long-term perspective. Rubbing someone's nose in defeat may be satisfying at the moment but more often than not creates enemies with long memories and a hunger for revenge. Allowing managers

Political Savvy

to save face in a defeat can help make them allies in the future.

Also, a long-term perspective can make losing easier to bear as illustrated by the true story in exhibit 41. Track some of the most successful movies and see how many times they were rejected before being picked up by another studio. Admittedly, most organizational life is not the same as Congress or Hollywood, but if initiatives for change are designed in a fail-functional mode, even a failure can become a successful step to eventual acceptance and implementation of an idea.

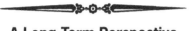

A Long-Term Perspective

A senator and his staff had been working long hours for several months toward passage of an important bill. When the bill finally came to the floor, it failed by a 51 to 45 vote. A reporter who had been following the bill went to the senator's office afterward. He was expecting to do a loser's locker room interview. When he got to the senator's office however, he heard a party going on. After checking twice to make sure that he was in the right place, he walked in. He said to one of the partying staffers, "Am I mistaken or didn't the bill you all worked so hard on just go down in defeat?" The happy staffer responded, "That's right." "Well then, why the party?" asked the reporter. The staffer remarked, "Sure we lost but this time it was only by six votes. Last year we lost by 15 votes, and three years ago we lost by 28 votes. We are really making progress!"

exhibit 41

SUMMARY OF CUSTOMIZING ATTEMPTS AT INFLUENCE

Once an initial strategy has been developed based upon political mapping and agenda linking, then specific tactics of strategy implementation can be brought to bear. Techniques for building momentum appropriate to a given culture can then be customized for greater effectiveness.

Customizing attempts at influence includes treating executive attention as a scarce resource. Idiosyncrasy management is a way of respecting individual differences and increasing the efficiency of the influence attempt. Managers can be included at several levels in the change initiative. Involvement, however, is a double-edged sword. It increases interaction and ownership, but it also serves as a source of detailed ammunition for anyone against the change. The Plan-Act Matrix can be useful in customizing an influence strategy based upon the amount of feedback available and the price of a mistake. Interpersonal diplomacy diminishes the creation of losers, fosters intelligent risk taking, and plays an important part in customizing any attempt at influence. Finally, adopting a long-term perspective makes it easier to spread credit, foster face-saving, and commit to a course of action different from the one you proposed.

Chapter 11

HANDLING THE MACHS

...[P]rinces who have achieved great things have been those who have given their word lightly, who have known how to trick men with their cunning, and who, in the end, have overcome those abiding by honest principles.

—Niccolo Machiavelli, *The Prince*

Part of what it means to be an ethical player is to help keep the organization ethical. Every company has its share of Machs. This chapter presents an orientation for dealing with Machs, which combines ways to identify them with a few basic counter measures.

For the sake of discussion, the active players have been sharply divided into two types, the Machs and the Savvy. As one journalist put it, "There are two kinds of people in the world. There are those who divide the world into two kinds of people, and there are those who don't." In reality, active players are spread out along a continuum, with the black hat, pure Mach anchoring one end and the white hat, pure Savvy anchoring the other.

As much as the mind wants to simplify the world by dividing it into good guys and bad guys, humans are too complex to be so easily stereotyped. In fact, brain research indicates that there is likely a Mach buried in each of us somewhere in the primitive part of the brain designed for survival. To paraphrase the philosopher Pogo, "We have met the Machs and they are us." The difference is that some managers learn to control this part of themselves while others give it free rein in the belief that "That's the way the world works." Some managers with a moral block have confessed that one of their concerns about becoming an active player comes from a fear that becoming active may release the Mach tendencies they have been controlling inside.

Despite this human complexity, it is still useful to discuss the Machs in pure terms. They represent an archetype that most people can readily understand. The pure Mach's view of the world was expressed earlier by George Orwell in exhibit 4. Pure Machs don't want power to help others or to get things done; they want power for its own sake.

Some people still believe the best way to handle Machs is to confront them directly about their motivations. The Savvy seldom take this approach for two reasons. First, it is almost impossible to prove motives. An example of what can happen when directly confronting a Mach is shown in exhibit 42. This example is based on an actual incident in which an executive widely viewed to be a Mach had someone transferred to a remote part of the organization. It makes the point that Machs generally have acceptable explanations to rationalize their behavior and who is to say they may not be right? It is usually fruitless and a waste of time to try to determine another person's true motivation.

Confronting a Mach

"Larry, I've held off speaking to you about this for some time because I don't like to question other people's motives, but transferring Harriet to El Paso was the last straw. I think what you did was disgraceful. The whole office knows Harriet was the brightest star we've had around here in years. I think you had her transferred because she was a threat to you. You're one ambitious S.O.B., Larry, who wants more than anything to be CEO. You're greedy as hell, the way you fight for more and more salary. Your status consciousness makes me sick, with your big fancy office, country club membership, company limo, and all those other perks. You turn my stomach and somebody had to tell you for your own good. There! I've finally said it. What do you have to say for yourself?"

"Craig, I'm shocked. Calm down, old buddy, and let's talk about this. Are you sure you're okay? I had no idea you felt this way. The Harriet transfer thing has really got you shook up. Sure I had Harriet transferred but not because I felt threatened by her. Harriet is good, yes, and it's because she's so good that I went out of my way to give her a tough assignment that would season her and make her even more valuable to the company.

"You called me ambitious. Well, certainly. That's why the organization hired me. Read the recruiting ad, Craig. It said they were looking for ambitious people to join a thriving company. So I did and so did you.

"You also said I want very much to be CEO. Well, that's true, too. I've been in the business for some time now, and I honestly believe I can see potential for this company as few others can. I long to make a significant contribution, and the CEO position is where I believe I can most help the shareholders and employees.

"The other thing you said was that I was greedy. Well, if you mean I'd like to have lots of money, then that's also true. My family means everything to me. Craig, I grew up poor. I want my family to have all the things I didn't. I want my kids to have the best possible education so they fully develop themselves and can be of service to society. My wife has struggled hard with me through many tough times, and now I want her to have the things I couldn't give her before.

"I think the last thing you said was that I was status conscious. Well, in a sense, I think you're right there also. Ever since I was a little kid, my parents wanted me to be somebody. You should see my mother's eyes light up when she comes into my office. She can't understand the work I do, but she feels I must be somebody if I have an office like this and a fancy company car. It makes her feel that all the years she sacrificed to pay for my education were really worth it. It makes her so proud.

"I'm sorry this comes across to you in such a negative way, Craig. I'm really beginning to worry about you. Are you sure there isn't something else that's really bothering you?"

exhibit 42

The second reason savvy managers don't dwell on someone's inner motivations is that such knowledge isn't really necessary to develop a viable game plan. The key information about Machs is their agendas, both public and private. It makes less difference to have a deep psychological understanding of why they are ambitious than to know that their behavior is predictable. The Savvy are interested in producing results for the organization, not in playing amateur psychiatrist to judge an individual's character.

Thus we come to the first principle for handling Machs.

Any force that is predictable can eventually be used to create beneficial results.

Obviously, if the force is in the direction that the savvy manager wants to go, using that force is relatively straightforward. But what if the force is in direct opposition to the savvy person's aims? It's in this situation that savvy artistry reaches its highest form.

There is a martial art that relies on the basic technique of

Handling the Machs

using an opponent's own force against himself—Akido. Savvy strategy is similar in many ways to Akido. They both are highly ethical and focus on the fundamental forces at play. Much about handling Machs in an organization can be learned on the mats in an Akido training hall.

Another analogy of using predictable opposition forces to reach a desired goal comes from the sport of sailing. By appropriately tacking, expert sailors use the wind that flows against them to help them reach their destination. Their course often zigzags and so does the Savvy's in handling the Machs. A manager in a brokerage firm on Wall Street gave an example of using the principle:

> *Several of us believed we needed to get rid of our stuffed shirt image and stop coasting on our past glories. We felt the firm should aggressively seek new business, become more focused on the customer, and create a down-to earth, roll-up-your sleeves image. While many shared our belief that such a move was vital to staying competitive, we were dead in the water. Two major principals in the firm were staunchly against such a change that in their minds would undermine the firm's long-standing prestige. The feeling was that their real opposition might stem from a possible threat of dethroning the old guard.*
>
> *We had all the logical debates. Each side brought reams of financial data and market analysis to bolster its position. But we were at a standstill. It wasn't until we took a different tack that the logjam was broken.*
>
> *We knew two things about one of the principals. He was feeling threatened by the new direction, and maybe because he was a first generation American from a poor immigrant family, he was particularly status conscious. He always went after whatever perks were available and then some. He had the best oak desk, the biggest office, the most expensive company car, and so forth.*
>
> *The one thing everybody knew about the second principal was that he loved Miami. He somehow arranged several business*

trips a year there even though we had no office on the east coast.

In putting two plus two together, we came up with an approach to put some tactical meat on the strategy bones. It included making the first principal the chairman of the firm. This was largely a ceremonial position since the executive committee made most of the key decisions, but it had high public visibility and did serve as a useful public relations role for the firm. Second, the direction in which we wanted to go called for branching out, and market research indicated a decent potential client base in Miami. So our strategy suggested opening up several new branch offices "closer to the customer," and the first one would be in Miami.

Well, no one knows for sure what really led to their decision, but the two principals appeared to go along reluctantly. Our Miami business is now solid and growing. The chairman has a good time hobnobbing with politicians, serving on prestigious boards, and speaking with the business press. He turned out to be rather good at it and he has helped enhance the image of the firm.

The general lesson from the Savvy is that the most constructive way to handle possible Machs is not to prove they are Machs nor to take them head on unless absolutely necessary. Instead, the best technique is to be creative about channeling their drives for the good of the organization.

Identifying Machs

Even if one is not an active player, a manager may still want to know who the Machs are, if only for the sake of self protection. There are several identifying marks that Machs typically display.

Grabbing credit is one of the hallmarks of true Machs. They generally have many more ways than others to associate themselves with anything that's seen as a success in the organization. Numerous examples occur daily in most companies.

Handling the Machs

One executive told how, when his firm's mailroom was successfully automated, the manager in Marketing went around telling others, "You know, I suggested that three years ago to the VP of Administration. I'm glad he finally acted on it."

But perhaps an even higher art form of the great Machs is their ability to keep blame away from themselves when something goes wrong. They will generally shunt it to two kinds of people. The easy ones are the known screw-ups. "Jason did it again. We couldn't get the product delivered because he wasn't on time with the resources we needed." The second kind are those perceived as direct competitors. This diversion of blame is a greater challenge to the Mach because competitors can retaliate. Therefore, it often takes the form of whispered remarks in safe places to executives who can affect careers. One executive commented on her experience:

> *I'll have to admit, Alex was pretty smooth about how he implicated me. His department fouled up on a key project and then I heard how he "accidentally" bumped into one of the senior executives and said, "It's really too bad about the Johnson Account mistake. We had our side all set up then Gloria's side failed to coordinate. I'm concerned. That's so unlike her. But she's been under a lot of stress lately. Maybe she's beginning to lose it." The next thing I knew, the senior executive called me into his office to have a "little chat,' about how I was feeling and asked if the pressure was getting to be too much for me. I was caught off guard because we had nothing to do with the foul-up; so, I blew my stack. All that accomplished was reinforcing the concern that maybe I couldn't handle the pressure. Alex must have gotten a pretty good laugh out of that one.*

While Machs may be ever present at official social gatherings, busy schmoozing and name dropping, many of them are actually loners. They often have few close friends in the organization unless it's someone higher up who is acting as a sponsor. Another common indicator of people with Mach tendencies is that superiors hold them in much higher esteem than do peers and subordinates. Machs focus so much of their attention on impressing the boss that they often ignore the views of others.

Readers can add their own indicators to this relatively short list. While almost every manager at times indulges in one or more of these behavior patterns, pure Machs show more of them more consistently.

Countering Mach Tactics

There are more ways than one might think to limit the Machs' dysfunctional effects. Nothing works for certain, and a sophisticated Mach can generally outmaneuver most strategies. However, there are tactics that can stop or at least inhibit a Mach from having free rein in an organization. One advantage here is the "pickpocket's syndrome." In some informal research, it was found that the easiest pockets to pick were those of the pickpockets themselves! They assume that they are the only ones going after the prey and often leave themselves wide open to someone trying to pick their pockets. It just doesn't occur to some Machs that there might be a savvy opponent outmaneuvering the maneuverer. A few basic tactics for countering Machs are now briefly discussed.

Shed Light on the Process

Machs enjoy working in the dark and in private, where they have the most room to maneuver. The classical smoke filled back room is one of their favorite habitats. Making the decision process more public and including more points of view can not only result in better decisions but also make the Mach's task more difficult. The Mach has to deal with more people and certain ploys are harder to pull off in the light of a public process. This is one beneficial use of a group setting.

Handling the Machs

Provide Opportunities for Self-Revelation

An expert Mach can easily deflect a direct confrontation. A more constructive tactic is allowing Machs to be caught at their own game. Exhibit 43 illustrates this general principle.

How They Catch Monkeys in Malaysia

Ever try to catch a monkey? Well, it's next to impossible. Try even the slightest move in their direction, and they scamper away. Their natural abilities of speed and intelligence make them a formidable challenge. Yet, they have one predictable trait—they are greedy. Knowing this, the natives have developed a unique approach. First, they get a coconut and some rice. Next, they bore a small hole just large enough to allow the monkey's slender fingers into the coconut. They then place rice into the hollowed-out coconut, stake it to the ground, and retreat to the bushes.

Soon a monkey comes down, rattles and smells the coconut, and slips his hand in for the free rice. To grab the food, the monkey must make a fist, which is bigger than the size of the tiny hole. The monkey struggles to get his fist of rice past the hole but can't. At this point, the natives come out from the bushes and walk toward the monkey. Rather than letting go and running away, the monkey wants the rice so badly that he refuses to part with even a grain. Chattering wildly but still holding on to the rice, the monkey is easily caught. As one native explained, We don't catch the monkey. The monkey catches himself."

exhibit 43

This principle was applied by a public utility director, except in his case grabbing credit replaces grabbing rice.

Janice was a vice president in our company who knew how to look good in her superiors' eyes. Her peers and subordinates felt

Political Savvy

she was incompetent and was only being seen favorably because she was skilled at taking credit for others' successes. Finally, after one particularly blatant incident of stealing credit, I got fed up. I restrained my impulse to go to Janice or upper management directly, for that could have backfired and might have been dismissed as jealousy on my part. By accident, I discovered another way to address the situation.

A particular project had been going quite well, thanks to the brilliant work of a number of dedicated professionals and lower level managers. It was a risky effort and Janice had distanced herself from it as if awaiting the outcome. The risk paid off, however, and the first set of successful results were likely to be presented at the next executive management meeting. If Janice was overly ambitious this would be too good an opportunity for her to pass up.

I was sitting in on a lower level meeting where the preliminary results were being discussed. It hit me that there might be a way to ensure credit went where it was due. I mentioned at the meeting that I was impressed with the results and thought it might be a good idea for several of the VPs to hear about them prior to the executive management meeting. They felt fine about the idea so I informally set up individual meetings with some of the VPs. Each meeting consisted of a lead engineer or manager giving the VP a brief preview of the project and its results prior to the executive management meeting. The VPs enjoyed the preview and several of the key professionals and managers got some deserved exposure. Janice was not on the list of those with whom we met.

Well, the executive management meeting took place and, when the status of the project came up, Janice was prepared. She immediately jumped in and, true to form, remarked about how much she had backed and supported the project. She spoke in terms of we, referring to herself and some of the lower level managers involved, and the role she played regarding them.

The VPs who had heard the briefings started to ask some detailed questions, to which Janice couldn't know the answers because of her lack of involvement. She tried to smooth over the situation with some general responses. However, a VP said he had spoken with one of the lead engineers and that Janice's responses differed. Janice was able to wiggle out of that tense moment, but from then on, things began to change. Several of the VPs knew Janice's name had never been mentioned in the informal briefings. While they didn't say anything, the mood of the meeting shifted. Janice gracefully backed off, but the damage had been done. A doubt had been created in the other VPs' minds and she had done it to herself. In future meetings, her statements received increased scrutiny. Eventually, for reasons unknown, she made a lateral move to a position in another company.

This is a prime example of the Akido approach. As long as behavior is predictable, there are often ways to create situations where Machs' own actions demonstrate their true colors. The savvy Malaysian natives might say, "Allow greedy monkeys and Machs to catch themselves."

A couple of familiar micro tactics are now in order as illustrations of how detailed the Mach's game can become.

Agenda Placement

Machs often have a good sense of where an agenda item should be placed in a given meeting. The best place for these items varies according to the culture of the organization and the nature of the meeting, but Machs know that the last items are often the easiest to put through. Executives are usually tired at the end of a long meeting and sometimes will agree quickly to any recommendation that sounds decent because they want to get the meeting over with and go home. Another good spot for railroading an item through is right before an agenda item known to be of great interest among those present. People are generally eager to dispense with agenda items standing in the way of one that they are itching to get to.

Some counter moves are to put the agenda item near the beginning of a long meeting or right after a break, or in some way to center the meeting around that particular agenda item. Machs themselves use the early placement or centering tactic to slow down items they don't want to see passed. They know it's easiest then to have a new idea scrutinized to death.

There are many other agenda placement tactics. The key point is that placement does have an impact and one should be conscious of where an issue is put on the agenda.

Tabling

Closely associated with agenda placement is expert use of tabling. Smart Machs go into a meeting prepared to use this tactic in case the idea they support starts to get into trouble.

They simply say something like, "Listen, folks, it seems we aren't getting closure here. Let's table the item for the moment and return to it." While the matter is tabled, they do some backroom work to shore up their position. A basic counter tactic is to be aware of this possibility and quickly respond with a remark like, "Wait a minute. This is an important issue and I think we should stay with it."

If one isn't prepared, Machs can whisk an issue out of the room and go to the next agenda item so quickly that one won't realize what's happening. Fortunately, the same tactic can be used by the Savvy when they see their issue getting caught up in dysfunctional group dynamics.

Rounded Performance Appraisal

While the last two counter tactics have been on a deliberately small scale, they show how minute influence tactics can become. The counter tactic of rounded appraisal is of an entirely different nature. It is a technique for the long run and may require a significant shift in the organization's culture. It is perhaps the best investment an organization can make to promote healthy politics while diminishing unhealthy politics.

Rounded appraisal means moving away from the traditional approach, which in some organizations is entirely from the top down. That is, the supervisor provides up to 100 percent of the performance appraisal which generally determines pay increases and bonuses. Such a system almost forces individuals to pay much more attention to impressing superiors and to care less about how peers, subordinates, or possibly even customers perceive their performance.

The heart of rounded performance appraisal, as the name suggests, is to solicit performance input from a broader range of perspectives. This form of appraisal, which many of the better managers already do intuitively, capitalizes on the power of convergent validity mentioned in earlier chapters. It involves seeking input from users or customers on the quality of the individual's performance, from peers on the individual as a team player, and from subordinates on the individual's leadership. The weight assigned to each of these inputs is generally agreed upon by the individual and the manager when goals are set at the beginning of the evaluation period. While it is relatively easy to look good from any one perspective, it is extremely difficult to look good simultaneously to subordinates, customers, peers, and bosses without actually being good. With rounded appraisals, Machs will find it considerably more difficult to grab credit from their peers or to tyrannize their subordinates while still looking great to their bosses.

Rounded appraisal is chock full of practical problems (such as bureaucracy, distortion by peers due to competition, or distortion by subordinates due to fear of retaliation), but it is a solid, long-term approach worth the investment. There is nothing that tears the heart out of an organization more than continually watching promotions and credit going to individuals who don't deserve them. No matter how great a company's vision is and no matter how inspiring management talks, if Machs get the rewards, employees will not give their commitment to the organization. Rounded appraisal limits an individual's ability to follow Mach tendencies without eventually being noticed by the organization.

SUMMARY ON HANDLING MACHS

Dividing active players into two polar extremes ignores the complexity of human beings, but it does allow for a more focused discussion. It's not fruitful to confront Machs directly and is generally not necessary. As long as a Mach's behavior is predictable, there is a good chance of developing a creative strategy to channel that force into beneficial directions.

While there is no sure way of identifying a Mach, some indications can be seen in persistent behaviors, such as grabbing credit, spreading blame, being a loner, and focusing on pleasing superiors.

Certain tactics are useful in countering Mach tendencies. Some of the major ones include: shedding more public light on the decision-making process, using Machs' own tendencies against themselves, and using rounded performance appraisals. These are a small but representative sample of counter tactics available to the Savvy and illustrate that one is not helpless when dealing with Machs.

PART FIVE

Summary and Conclusions

These cases illustrate what is perhaps the greatest benefit of power and political activity in organizations — it is the organizational politicking which facilitates organizational change and adaptation to the environment.

—Jeffrey Pfeffer, *Power in Organizations*

Chapter 12

SUMMARY

Regardless of how managers use power, the fact remains that without it they are incapable of achieving anything of significance for themselves, other people, the company, or society at large.

—Diane Tracy, *The Power Pyramid*

We've covered a lot of ground in the past eleven chapters. This chapter lists the basic points in two ways. First, they are listed as steps in becoming more politically savvy. This list pretty much follows the flow and language of the book and should serve as a quick reference guide. References at the end of the chapter will lead the reader back into the text, where the points were discussed earlier.

The second type of summary results from asking individual managers to describe these steps in their own terms. Their comments often were of the form: "What this really means is..." or "In other words..." These in-other-words-type of remarks are useful contrasts to the more conceptual language of the book and are included alongside each step.

Political Savvy

> **Political Savvy**
>
> **Ethically
> building a critical mass of support
> for an idea
> you care about**

There are only two major points in this book:

A. Choose to become an active, ethical player.

"Don't be afraid to lead."

B. Work the human system.

"Change doesn't happen by itself."

Remembering these two points alone would be sufficient for most people to start developing their own savvy skills. The additional points that follow help only to elaborate them.

STEPS TO BECOMING POLITICALLY SAVVY

A. Choose to Become an Active, Ethical Player.

1. Put the organization first.

"You're not in business for yourself."

2. Understand the assumptions underlying your own political style.

"You can't choose the right style if you don't know the options."

Summary

3. **Believe strongly in your change initiative.**

   "If you don't really care, why should anybody else?"

4. **Regard your career as an outcome, rather than as a goal.**

   "Work for the greater good, but don't be stupid."

5. **Play above board.**

   "You don't have to cheat to win."

6. **Legitimize the task.**

   "Make it okay to strategize."

   a. **Do not be stopped by the moral and technical blocks.**

   "It's alright to jump into the fray; being right is not enough."

   b. **Treat the organization as a human system, rather than just as a rational one.**

   "Machines are neat; organizations are messy."

B. **Work the Human System.**

   1. **Map the territory.**

   "Learn the true nature of the jungle you're working in."

   a. **Identify the key players.**

   "Know who has their fingers in the pie."

b. Gauge their power and influence.

"Understand the real pecking order."

c. Determine their position—whether they are for or against—and the degree of their applied influence.

"Figure out who's on the bandwagon, who's on the fence, and who's going the other way."

d. Rate the stability of their applied influence.

"Know whose mind is still open and whose is already made up."

e. Assess significant relationships among them.

"Tune in to the local soap opera."

2. Develop a strategy.

"Think, and be smart about your approach."

a. Form a strategy coalition.

"You're not that smart by yourself."

b. Identify the multiple agendas.

"Find out what's on people's minds, and read between the lines."

c. Brainstorm for win-win possibilities.

"Be creative about connecting what different people want."

d. Link agendas.

"Construct bridges between the fiefdoms."

Summary

e. Build an action coalition.

> *"Give people reasons to work together."*

f. Follow the credibility paths.

> *"'Trust is a smooth highway, distrust a rocky road."*

3. Use savvy tactics and techniques.

> *"If it's important enough to fight for, do it right."*

a. Understand the culture.

> *"Learn the ropes so you don't trip up."*

b. Build momentum.

> *"A new idea needs a lot of support before it will work."*

c. Utilize the 51 percent guide.

> *"Take it one step at a time, and gear each meeting for success."*

d. Design the purpose and timing of group meetings.

> *"Don't expect group meetings to do the work."*

e. Use systematic informality.

> *"Drop by on schedule."*

f. Play above board.

> *"Don't hide what you're trying to do."*

g. **Employ the many-few-many-few technique.**

> *"Involve lots of people, but don't lose control."*

h. **Customize attempts at influence.**

> *"Know who you're really talking to."*

i. **Treat executive attention as a scarce resource.**

> *"Time is more valuable than money, so don't waste it."*

j. **Utilize idiosyncrasy management.**

> *"Do it their way."*

k. **Determine the appropriate involvement level for each player.**

> *"Don't send the same invitation to everyone."*

l. **Choose the appropriate plan-act mix.**

> *"Play it by ear only when you can clearly hear the music."*

m. **Employ interpersonal diplomacy.**

> *"Help others save face."*

4. **Handle the Machs.**

> *"At least make it harder for the bad guys."*

a. **Identify possible Machs.**

> *"Look to see who might be hiding in the weeds."*

Summary

b. Open up on the decision process.

"Put the manipulators in a minority."

c. Provide opportunities for Machs to reveal themselves.

"help allow greed to self-destruct."

d. Move toward rounded performance appraisal.

"Use the whole team to spot Machs before they develop."

STEPS AND ASSOCIATED TEXT REFERENCES

A. See chapters 1-3.
   1. See pp. 49, 112-113.
   2. See chapter 2.
   3. See pp. 48-49.
   4. See pp. 46, 48-49.
   5. See pp. 32-34, 48, 141-144.
   6. See pp. 19-21, 27-44, 53, 79.
      a. See pp. 30-34, 35-44.
      b. See pp. 39-41.
B. See chapters 5-11.
   1. See chapter 5.
      a. See p. 67.
      b. See p. 68.
      c. Ibid.
      d. Ibid.
      e. Ibid.

   2. See chapters 6-7.
      a. See chapter 6.
      b. See pp. 96-98.

c. See pp. 99-101.
d. Ibid.
e. See pp. 95-96, 102-103.
f. See pp. 103-106.

3. See chapters 9-11.
   a. See chapter 8.
   b. See chapter 9.
   c. See pp. 128-133.
   d. See pp. 133-139.
   e. See pp. 139-140.
   f. See pp. 141-144.
   g. See pp. 144-149.
   h. See chapter 10.
   i. See pp. 154-156.
   j. See pp. 157-162.
   k. See pp. 162-168.
   l. See pp. 168-174.
   m. See pp. 174-181.

4. See chapter 11.
   a. See pp. 190-192.
   b. See p. 192.
   c. See pp 193-195.
   d. See pp. 196-197.

Chapter 13

CONCLUSIONS

The act of commitment is to decide to fulfill the purpose of the job and not to wait until conditions are more supportive. The commitment needs to be made regardless of who our boss is, or how the business is going, or how alone we seem to be in our purpose.

—Peter Block, *The Empowered Manager*

This book has been about how leaders operate behind-the-scenes to make change happen in their organizations. As we end, there are several points worth special attention because they relate to the context of applying political savvy concepts, strategies, and tactics in organizational life. A few points are cautions and a few are challenges.

First, the cautions. The initial caution has to do with the risk of overstrategizing. This point was addressed previously but it needs further emphasis. Once one legitimizes the task and gets comfortable with conscious strategizing, it can become absorbing and even fun in its own right. There is no end to the

Political Savvy

number of moves and counter moves that can be considered. As a result, it's possible to get caught up in trivia and to overcalculate. Overcalculating occurs when the game-like nature of the activity takes over. For example, there were managers who expressed ethical concerns about organization politics but took a wrong turn when they worked on the Milford Case. They got so caught up in wanting to win for Alice that they were willing to use the unethical information. When asked to reconcile their original concerns with their actual behavior, most didn't know how to respond. Those who did said things like, "It just seemed to make sense at the time."

Responsible strategizing means keeping it as a means to an ethical end and not as an end in itself. In order to avoid getting carried away with trivia and the game-like aspects of strategizing for its own sake, it's important to keep uppermost in one's mind why he or she is trying to contribute to the organization in the first place. Political savvy is important, but it is only one dimension of overall effectiveness.

The next caution is concerned with speaking to others in the organization about political savvy concepts. Leadership behind the-scenes by its very nature has been an informal activity occurring in the background of organizational life. Bringing something that is normally unseen and in the background into the visible foreground has value but also can create difficulties.

The intuitively Savvy generally don't have labels for their behavior, particularly when they are unaware of their natural skills. Even if they did, many of them would prefer that this topic be kept out of the limelight for the very reason that it is not a limelight activity.

Most people, whether savvy or unsavvy, have not consciously made the distinction between political savvy behavior and manipulation. Also, most organizations strongly believe that they should be rational entities where technical merit is sufficient. As a result, many companies have a cultural taboo about discussing organization politics. It's not considered appropriate behavior in polite organizational conversation. Therefore,

Conclusions

when the topic is brought up, there is often an uneasiness in the air.

Until working the human system has been accepted by others as a legitimate activity, one should use caution when speaking about political savvy strategies and tactics. Under these conditions he or she will likely fare better to operate by these principles than to talk about them.

These cautions can be summarized as follows: avoid getting too caught up in strategizing and be aware that speaking about political savvy concepts, strategies, and techniques can make many people, even the Savvy, uneasy.

With these cautions in mind, we move to three key challenges for those who want to increase their leadership abilities. All three relate to development. Exhibit 44 represents one version of an ancient proverb about wisdom. At the lowest level are the Ignorant who don't know what they don't know and thus can't even begin to develop. At the next level are the Naturals and the Learners. Naturals don't know what they know. They perform beautifully but generally can't explain how they do it. Learners know what they don't know. They can't perform as well as the Naturals, but they are aware of what it will take. At the top are the wise Developers who know what they know. They perform as well as the naturals, plus they can coach others to develop similar skills.

The first challenge is for the Learners, individuals who have picked up this book because they are aware that there are aspects about influencing organizations that they may not know. The challenge stems from the basic limitations of any book. The way political savvy has been described is not how it is played out in organizations. Therefore, it would be a mistake to assume that understanding political savvy concepts means one is politically savvy. In a sense, this book is like a dissected rose whose component parts have been segmented, labeled, and conceptualized into a systematic order. While adding to knowledge, a dissected rose doesn't look as pretty or smell as sweet as the original. Taking a whiff of the written formula for rose fragrance will smell more like ink than rose.

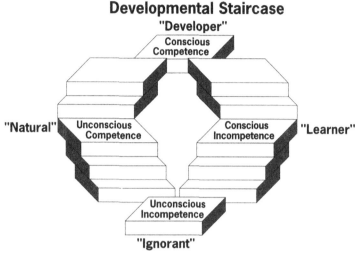

exhibit 44

The political savvy concepts discussed here represent a printed series of savvy dance steps. The challenge is to continually practice and personally integrate the steps so that the knowledge will eventually translate into practical wisdom. Knowledge of the steps is very valuable in developing one's savvy skills. Such knowledge is, however, a far cry from doing the dance itself.

The second challenge is for the Naturals. For many people, leadership is about getting things done. If directions are being set, priorities are being established, and people are being motivated, then they are performing their leadership role.

Naturals often stop at this level of understanding leadership. At a higher level, however, another aspect of leadership becomes even more critical. Leadership in the near term is making things happen. In the long term, leadership is developing people. The ultimate responsibility of a leader is not just to make things happen today but to increase the organization's capaci-

Conclusions

ty to make things happen tomorrow. The best leaders accomplish this by developing others to become leaders.

Naturals often fail to contribute on this score. While the intuitively Savvy can influence the organization, they frequently don't help others develop savvy skills. Claiming their actions are common sense, far too many Naturals end up hoarding their skills. It may be unintentional, but leaving their abilities unexamined limits their own movement up the developmental staircase.

The material in this book has tried to codify and make accessible some of the attitudes and behaviors of the intuitively Savvy. As various points were covered, many readers probably had feelings of "I knew that" or "I already do that. I just never called it anything." Such feelings indicate areas where they are Naturals. Conceptualizing behaviors and attaching labels to them is an essential part of turning unconscious competence into conscious competence. The challenge to the Naturals is to continue this process and further articulate their skills in ways that make them more transferable to others. Only then will they contribute at the highest levels of leadership.

The final challenge is about the future. While political savvy strategies have been used throughout human history, there is reason to believe they will be even more needed in the years ahead.

As much as this book has been about organization politics, it has been more about organizational change. Nothing in our past is likely to prepare us to handle the sheer amount and diversity of change coming our way in the future. As environments change more rapidly, organizations will have a harder time keeping up. Each environmental change must be interpreted, possible responses must be developed, and then agreement must be reached before the organization can successfully adapt. In an era of increasing global competition, the response time available to an organization is shrinking. Traditional bureaucratic processes become grossly inefficient under conditions of rapid change.

Political Savvy

Some organizations will look for charismatic limelight leaders to make quick autocratic decisions. Enough will be successful with the simplistic approach to perpetuate the myth of the single great leader solution. However, the issues will be more complex than a single person's mind size and looking for the one person who will save the company puts the organization's fate more in the hands of luck than intelligence.

The truly successful organizations will be those that have worked hard to create leaders at all levels in the organization. Not the kind of leaders who push only for their own views, but the kind of leaders who know how to take the initiative and rapidly forge a consensus for action. This ability to develop a consensus among diverse individuals lies at the heart of political savvy skills.

These challenges are but a few of the reasons to take a more serious interest in developing your own political savvy skills. Develop them for the issues you care about in the organization. Develop them for the people you care about who are working so hard on these issues. Develop them for your organization so that its capacity to change is increased. But most of all develop them for yourself because it is very difficult to become more politically savvy without also becoming a more developed human being.

Sources for Epigraphs & Exhibits

Lord Acton in *The Oxford Dictionary of Quotations*, I:2. 2d Ed. London: Oxford University Press, 1966. Or "Letter to Bishop Creighton," in *Animal, Vegetable, Mineral*, NY, 1972.

Aristotle in the *Transformational Leader*, 121. Edited by N. M. Ticky and M. A. Devanna. New York: Wiley, 1986.

Block, Peter. *The Empowered Manager*, 65-66. San Francisco: Jossey-Bass, 1987.

Buskirk, Richard H. *Frontal Attack, Divide & Conquer: The Fait Accompli, 5118 Other Tactics Managers Must Know*, 11. New York: Wiley, 1989.

Friedel, Egon in Joachim E. Berendt's *The Jazz Book: From Ragtime to Fusion*, 381. Chicago: Lawrence Hill Books, 1982.

Friedenberg, Edgar Z. *Coming of Age in America*, 36. New York, 1965.

James, Henry. *Selected Letters*, 181. Edited by Leon Edel. New York: Farrar, Straus and Cudsky, 1955.

Kakabadse Andrew, and Christopher Parker. *Power, Politics, and Organizations*, 95. New York: Wiley, 1985.

Kotter, John P. *Power and Influence: Beyond Formal Authority*, 3. New York: Free Press, 1985.

Kotter, J.P., and P. Lawrence. *Mayors in Action*. New York: Wiley, 1974.

Lee Hecht Harrison, Inc. "Partners in Career Transition Management." Advertisement in *Human Resource Executive* (April 1990): 14.

Lincoln, Abraham in *The Oxford Dictionary of Quotations*. 2d Ed. London: Oxford University Press, 1966.

Machiavelli, Niccolo. *The Prince*, 51, 99. New York: Penguin Books, 1976.

MacMillan, Ian C. *Strategy Formulation: Political Concepts*, xiii. St. Paul: West, 1978.

McClelland, David C. Power: The Inner Experience, 254. New York: Wiley, 1975.

Mead, Margaret. *The Wagon and the Star: A Study of American Community Initiative with Muriel Brown*, 187. Chicago: Rand McNally, 1966.

Moss Kanter, Rosabeth. *When Giants Learn to Dance: Mastering the Challenges of Strategy, Management, and Careers in the 1990's*. In Allan R. Cohen and David L. Bradford's Influence Without Authority, 1. New York: John Wiley & Sons, 1990.

Orwell, George. *1984*, 166, 216-217. New York: New American Library, 1984.

Pfeffer, Jeffrey. *Power in Organizations*, XI, 337. Massachusetts: Pittman Publishing, 1981.

Quinn, Robert E. *Beyond Rational Management: Meeting the Paradoxes and Competing Demands of High Performance*, 1. San Francisco: Jossey-Bass, 1988.

Sources for Epigraphs

Sapolsky, Harvey. *The Polaris System Development*, Massachusetts: Harvard University Press, 1972. In Jeffrey Pfeffer's *Power in Organizations*, 335-337. Massachusetts: Pitman Publishing, 1981.

Tracy, Diane. *The Power Pyramid: How to Get Power by Giving It Away*, 11. New York: William Morrow & Co., 1990.

Urquart, Sir Brian. *Time*. (December 5, 1988): 50.

Further Readings

There is a wide range of books related to organization politics. Some are theoretical; some are practical. A few are both. The books mentioned here are recommended for those who wish to delve further into this fascinating topic.

While experience is the best teacher, written works can help guide that experience. The first section lists books which address important dimensions of power. The next section contains collections of articles. The third section represents books for those with an intellectual bent. The final section lists books about tips and tactics, as promised in the preface.

The Prince, Nicolo Machiavelli, New York: Penguin Books, 1976, 138 pages.

One of the first written treatises on the exercise of power, Machiavelli was less interested in the ethics of politics than in its practice. His work was first translated into English in 1640 and has been reviled more for its morality than praised for its reality over the centuries. The book summarizes his observations and advice.

Power and Influence: Beyond Formal Authority, John P. Kotter, New York: Free Press, 1985, 198 pages.

This book demonstrates how power and influence lie at the core of leadership. It shows why the changing nature of work requires leadership throughout the organizations. The author pioneered one of the first courses in organizational power at Harvard Business School. His latter books, The Leadership Factor (1988) and A Force For Change (1990) are also excellent and use today's corporate leaders as examples.

Power: The Inner Experience, David C. McClelland, New York: Wiley, 1975, 359 pages.

A fine work on the psychology of power. Based upon a series of research studies by the author, it discusses the basic power motive as the need to have impact. He links different power orientations with Freud's stages of personality development. This is an indispensable book to anyone interested in understanding their own power motive. There is also an intriguing chapter on how men and women relate to power differently.

The Tao of Power: Lao Tzu's Classic Guide to Leadership, Influence, and Excellence, A new translation of the Tao Te Ching by R.L. Wing, New York: Doubleday, 1986, 81 pages.

A modern translation of a Chinese classic. Words and 20th century meaning of a book written at about 500 B.C. It provides a good overview of the Eastern paradox of action through strategic non-action and leadership through flexibility rather than force.

Managing with Power; Politics and Influence in Organizations, Jeffrey Pfeffer, Boston: Harvard Business School Press; 1992 in hard cover, 1994 paperback. 391 pages.

Probably the best book in terms of depth and breadth on the topic. Densely packed. Not necessarily an easy read, but well worth the investment. You will come away deeply grounded in this intriguing topic.

Further Readings

The Empowered Manager: Positive Political Skills at Work, Peter Block, San Francisco: Jossey-Bass, 1991, 244 pages.

Aimed at middle managers, this book combines much of modern leadership theory and practice into useful guidelines. It's one of the few organization development books that directly tries to come to terms with the realities of organization politics. It would be most useful to those who work in departments characterized by positive trust levels.

The Power Principle, Blaine Lee, Fireside Publishing, 1998.

Shows how Stephen Covey's work, which includes the very popular "Seven Habits of Highly Effective People" and "Principled Leadership" relate to the Political Savvy arena.

Strategy Formulation: Political Concepts, Ian C. MacMillan, Minnesota: West, 1978, 157 pages.

An instructive text about organizational politics as it affects business planning. Its discussion of how political structures evolve in organizations is particularly valuable.

Influence Without Authority, Allan R. Cohen and David L. Bradford, New York: John Wiley & Sons, 1990, 305 pages.

An excellent book based on the philosophy that managers' responsibilities exceed their official authority. It offers influence approaches to create alliances that are inherently ethical.

The System Made Me Do It; A Life Changing Approach to Office Politics., Susan Osborn, Lifethread Publications, 1997, 176 pages.

One of the better new books that illustrates how ethics and politics can be used to reframe work life in a positive way.

Getting To Yes: Negotiating Agreement Without Giving In, Roger Fisher and William Ury, New York: Houghton Mifflin, 1981, 160 pages.

Valuable reading to implement the savvy strategy of linking agendas. One-on-one negotiating lies at the heart of creating an action coalition. This book is one of the best on the topic.

ANTHOLOGIES

Power and Politics in Organizations (The International Library of Management), Cynthia Hardy (Editor), Dartmouth Publications, 1995.

A pricey, but broad spectrum coverage of the political dimension of organization life. For those deeply interested in full coverage of the topic.

Power In Organizations, Edited by Mayer N. Zald, Tennessee: Vanderbilt University Press, 1970, 328 pages.

A series of scholarly articles on organizational power. In particular see contributions by Charles Perrow, James D. Thompson, and Peter Blau.

Power, Politics, and Organizations, Edited by Andrew Kakabadse and Christopher Parker, Chichester, England: John Wiley & Sons, 1984, 217 pages.

Further Readings

A variety of perspectives on power dynamics in organizations. This collection of articles covers concepts, applications and organizational change issues.

SCHOLARLY BOOKS THAT VIEW ORGANIZATIONS AS POLITICAL SYSTEMS

A Behavioral Theory of the Firm, R.M. Cyert and J.G. March, Englewood Cliffs, New Jersey: Prentice-Hall, 1963.

The Bureaucratic Phenomenon, M. Crozier, Chicago: University of Chicago Press, 1964.

Organizations in Action, J.D. Thompson, New York: McGraw Hill, 1967.

Power and Politics in Organizations, S.B. Bacharach and E.J. Lawler, San Francisco: Jossey-Bass, 1980.

TIPS AND TACTICS

The following books address micro-politics. They address numerous interpersonal tactics represented and are particularly useful in understanding moves associated with Machs.

Winning Office Politics, Andrew DuBrin, Englewood Cliffs, New Jersey: Prentice-Hall, 1990, 322 pages.

Tips for acquiring support from boss, peers, etc. Interactive in focus and emphasis is on gaining advantage.

Work Would Be Great If It Weren't For the People; Ronna and Her Evil Twin's Guide to Making Office Politics Work For You, Ronna Lichtenberg, Hyperion, 1998. 256 pages.

Humorous with valuable suggestions for turning individual agendas into common goals.

Frontal Attack, Divide & Conquer, The Fait Accompli, & 118 Other Tactics Managers Must Know, Richard Buskirk, New York: John Wiley & Sons, 1989, 237 pages.

Describes a long list of deceptive tactics used in organization politics.

Cubicle Warfare: Self Defense Strategies for Today's Hypercompetetive Workplace, Blaine Pardoe, Prima Publishing, 1997.

Countermoves to deal with the micro tactics of the "Machs" in daily office life.

Power: How to Get It, How to Use It, Michael Korda, New York: Ballantine Books, 1975, 305 pages.

A bestseller in its time, this book ranges from basic philosophies of power in human history to how power players arrange office furniture.

Body Politics: How to Get Power With Class, Julius Fost, New York: Tower Publications, 1980, 224 pages.

Micro tactics on how nonverbal cues such as body posture communicate impressions of power.

The Gentle Art of Verbal Self-Defense, Suzette Haden Elgin, New Jersey: Prentice-Hall, 1983, 292 pages.

Countermeasures to verbal power assaults in the workplace.

The Dilbert Principle, Scott Adams, Penguin Books, 1997

A comic strip view with some serious points related to politics as only Dilbert could.

The Politics of E-Mail, Harvard Business Review, April, 1998

A good, short commentary of this pervasive technology has entered into the dynamics of modern organization politics..

Index

A

Achievement needs, 28
Acting, customizing mix of planning and, 167-173
Action coalition, 92-95
    agenda linking and, 102-113
        chit system and, 102-103, 104, 180
        following credibility paths and, 103-109, 172
        political savvy versus professional lobbying in, 109-111
Action orientation
    political style and, 9, 10-21
    on Political Style Grid, 10-12
Acton, Lord, 27, 28, 31
Advisor style, 11, 16, 22
Affiliation needs, 28
Agenda linking, 95-113
    action coalition and, 102-113
    brainstorming for win-win possibilities in, 99-101
    in Chromium Project, 97-102
    definition of political savvy based on, 111-113
    identifying multiple agendas in, 96-98
Agenda placement tactics, 195
Agenda setting, 90
Akido approach, 189, 194-195
Alliances. See Coalitions, developing
Anecdotal evidence, executives need for, 139
Applied influence on OMPT Political Data Sheet, 68, 69
Appraisal, rounded performance, 196-197
Aristotle, 63
Assumptions, OPMT and testing of, 72
Attention, OPMT for directing, 73
Attitude, savvy, 53-54

B

Bias, political style and, 22
Blame, Machiavellians' diversion of, 191
Blind spot, political. See Political blind spot
Block, Peter, 213
Brainstorming, 172
    for win-win possibilities, 99-101
Bureaucracy, protector style leading to, 14
Burnout, 18, 180
Buskirk, Richard H., 153

C

Career
    long-term orientation and, 180-181
    Savvy versus Mach view of, 48
    Cautions regarding political savvy, 213-215
Challenges in use of political savvy, 215-216
Change
    challenge of organizational, 214-215
    as a destructive process, 84-85
    resistance to, 84-85, 130-131
    See also Momentum for change, building
Changeability of player's stance on OMPT Political Data Sheet, 68, 69
Charisma, xvii, 88
Chit system, 102-103, 104, 180
Chromium Project, 54-60
    agenda linking in, 97-102
    identifying agendas of key players and, 97-98
    brainstorming for win-win possibilities in, 99-101
    developing levels of coalition in, 89-93
    mapping political territory in, 70-74
    Organization Politics Map of, 71, 72-75, 104, 105
    official finalization of decision on, 137-138
    playing above board in, 141-142
Chrysler Corporation, 87
Coalitions, developing, 83-92
    advantages of, 85-89
    levels of coalitions, 89-92

OPMT and identification of coalition levers, 75
See also Agenda linking
"Colliding colleagues" syndrome, 155
Communication
    complexity of process of, 129
    effect of distrust on, 107
    with executives, 154-155
    informal, 15
Competitors, influence on validity of idea, 161
Confrontations with Machiavellians, 185-188
Consensus in decision making, 144-145
Consultant level of involvement, 166
Consultants, OPMT for maximizing contributions of, 75-77
Convergent validity, 85-86, 160-61, 195
Credibility
    executives' reliance on, 161-162
    playing above board and, 141-142, 149
Credibility paths, following, 103-108, 172
Credit
    Machiavellians' ability to grab, 190, 191-193
    spreading, 174-175, 180
Culture, organization, 119-124, 164
Customizing influence, 153-183
    executive attention as strategic resource in, 154-157, 179
    idiosyncrasy management in, 157-159
    interpersonal diplomacy in, 174-182
    involvement levels in, 162-168
    planning and acting mix in, 168-174
Cynic style, 11, 12

D

Data, executives' need for, 159
Decision making, 134-139
    consensus in, 144
    exploratory meeting and, 135-136
    many-few-many-few technique of, 144-149, 164
    official finalization of, 137-139
    shedding light on process of, 192
    Snowflake Theory of strategic decisions, xvi
Developmental staircase, 215-218

Diplomacy, interpersonal, 174-181
Distribution lists, placement on, 163-164
Distrust, effect on communication of, 107-110
Downward leadership, xiii
Dysfunctional politics, 42

E

Ego
    political savvy and ego needs, 132
    sensitivity to organization culture and, 121
Ends-justify-the-means method, 33-34, 108-109
Environment, plan-act matrix and, 168-174
Errors, cost of making, 168, 169, 171
Ethical alliance, benefits of, 85-89.
See also Coalitions, developing Ethical influence, 31, 32
Ethical situations, 32-34
Ethics
    coalitions and enhanced ethicalness, 87
    definition of political savvy based on, 112
    loyalist style and, 18 *see* Responsible Style
    playing above board and, 141-144
Executive attention as strategic resource, 154-157, 179
Executives
    choosing right timing with, 157-159
    individual requirements for validity of, 158-161
    responding to individual styles of processing of, 157-162
Exploratory group meetings, 134-137

F

Face-saving, fostering, 176-177, 180
"Fail-functional" design of a half-step, 172
Fatalist style, 11, 13, 22
Fear, resistance to change and, 130-131
Feedback, environmental, 168-173
51 percent guide, 128-134, 149, 156, 165, 172
Finalizing a decision, 137-139
Finesse
    Mach versus Savvy use of, 49
    resistance to change and, 129

Index

Five Basic Questions Sheet, OPMT, 64-68
Foot-shooting actions, 121-123
Formal oral presentations, 163-164
Founding Fathers, 19
Friedel, Egon, 7
Friedenberg, Edgar, 27, 31
Functional politics, 43
FYI (For Your Information), 163

G

Gracious losing, 176-180
Gracious winning, 175-176
Grapevine, organizational, 15, 49
Group setting, use of, 133-139, 149
    differences in processing styles and, 157
    initial exploration and, 135-136
    to shed light on decision process, 192

H

Half-steps, carefully planned, 172
Hepburn, Katherine, 176
Hitler, Adolf, 46
Human nature in organizations, assumptions about, 178-179
Human system, working the, 85, 86, 140, 203-206.
    See also Agenda linking; Coalitions, developing; Customizing influence;
    Momentum for change, building; Organization Politics Mapping Technique (OPMT)
Human systems, organizations as, 37, 39-40, 91

I

Iacocca, Lee, 87
Idiosyncrasy management, 157-158
Influence
    chit system and, 102-104, 180
    coalitions and, 88-89
    as continuum, 31
    51 percent guide and, 128-134, 149, 156, 165, 172

    of key players, 67
    manipulation versus, 31-34
    occurring outside formal group meetings, 139
    of Savvy versus Mach, 46-47
    See also Customizing influence
Informal communications, 15
Informality, systematic, 139-141, 149, 155, 156, 158, 164
Informal networking, 90
Informal oral presentations, 164
Information level of coalition, 89-91, 93
Information processing
    individual styles of, 157-158
    timing and, 158-159
Initiative, political styles oriented toward, 11, 17-21
Integrity, 18, 30, 47-48, 179.
See also Ethics Interest Grid, 41-43
Interpersonal diplomacy, 174-181
Interpersonal skills, xv, 111- 112, 174-175
Intuitive judgements, quantifying, 68-69
Involvement (inclusion), tactical use of, 162-167
    downsides of, 167-168

J

James, Henry, 48

K

Kakabadse, Andrew, 95
Kanter, Rosabeth Moss, 127
Key players, 67
    action level of coalition and access to, 91-92
    personal relationships among, 67-68
    win-win possibilities and personal agendas of, 101-102
Kotter, John P., 3, 90, 155

L

Lawrence, P., 155
Leadership
    behind the-scenes, xiii-xviii

Index

    coalitions providing, 89-90
    development of, in others, 217
    downward, xi limelight, xiii, 5-6
    by Naturals, challenge of, 217-218
    political savvy as key dimension of, xiii, 5-6
Leader style, 11-21
Learners on developmental staircase, challenge for, 215-216
Lee Hecht Harrison, Inc., 119
Legitimization of task, coalitions and, 86
Limelight leadership, xiii-xiv, 5-6
Lincoln, Abraham, 33
Lobbying, political savvy versus professional, 109-111
Loners, Machiavellians as, 46, 191
Long-term orientation, adopting, 180-181
Losing, gracious, 177-180

M

McClelland, David C., 1, 28
Machiavelli, Niccolo, 16, 84, 185
Machiavellians
    coalition's advantage over, 90
    distinction between the Savvy and the, 45-49, 112
    downsides of inclusion of, 167-168
    ends-justify-the-means method and, 32, 108
    handling, 185-198
        with confrontation, 186-188
        countering tactics of, 192-198
        with creative channeling, 190-192
    identifying, 190-192
    interest of, 41-42, 44
    interpersonal diplomacy and, 174, 175
    systematic informality used by, 141
    tactical use of involvement by, 162
    world view of, 186
Machiavellian style, 11, 16-17, 21
MacMillan, Ian C., 81
Management By Walking Around (MBWA), 5, 90, 140-141
Managers
    as devices for processing information, 157
    ego and sensitivity to organization culture of, 121

relationships established over careers of, 90-91
technically oriented, 37
use of term, xvii
Maneuverability, coalitions and, 87-89
Manipulation, 30-34, 47
Many-few-many-few technique, 144-149, 164
Martyr syndrome, 42
Mead, Margaret, 83, 88
Mental blocks moral block, 28-34, 108, 186
rational block, 35-41, 108
Milford Steel Company Case. See Chromium Project
Mistakes, costs of making, 168, 169, 170
Momentum for change, building, 127-150
percent guide for, 129-133, 149, 156, 164, 172
group settings, use of, 132-138, 149, 158
many-few-many-few technique for, 144-149, 164
playing above board for, 141-144
systematic informality for, 139-141, 149, 156, 158, 165
Moral block, 28-34, 108, 186
manipulation versus influence and, 30-34
Moral dilemma, 33-34
Motivation
determining another person's, 186-188
rationalist approach to, 39

N

Naturals, challenge for the, 216-217

Needs
achievement and affiliation, 28
ego, political savvy and, 133
power, 28-30
Networking
informal, 90
old boy network, 74
1984 (Orwell), 29
Norms, organizational, 123-24, 165. *See also* Organization culture

Index

O

Observer level of involvement, 165-166
Official finalization, group meetings for, 137-139
Old boy network, 74
Oral presentations, use of, 164-166
Organization(s)
    building momentum for entire, 144-149
    human nature in, assumptions about, 179-180
    rationalist versus savvy perspective on, 36-40, 91
Organizational change, challenge of, 213-214, 218
Organizational grapevine, 11, 15
Organization culture
    definition of, 119
    knowing, 119-24
    norms in formal oral presentation and, 164-165
    working with, 120-121
Organization influence on OPMT Political Data Sheet, 68, 69
Organization politics
    action orientation toward, 9, 10
    cultural taboo about discussing, 214-215
    Cynic's view of, 12
    definition of, 41-42
    dysfunctional versus functional, 41-42
    Leader's view of, 18-20
    moral block and avoidance of, 28
    political style and assumptions about, 22-24
    popular beliefs about, 8-9
    rational block and avoidance of, 39-41
    Speculator's view of, 15
Organization Politics Map, OPMT, 66
    for Chromium Project, 71, 72-75, 104, 105
    coalitions and validity of, 85-86
    creation of, 64, 66, 70-71
Organization Politics Mapping Technique (OPMT), 63-79, 131
    advantages of, 73-74
    caveats about, 75-78
    for Chromium Project, 64-74
    purpose of, 78
    reluctance to use, 76
    steps in, 64-71

Five Basic Questions Sheet, OPMT, 64, 67-68
Organization Politics Map, creation of, 64, 66, 70-71
OPMT Political Data Sheet, compiling, 64, 65, 68-69
Orwell, George, 29-30, 186
Outside resources, OPMT for maximizing contributions of, 74
Overload, 159
Overmapping with OPMT, 76-78
Overstrategizing, risk of, 213-214
Ownership, involvement Ievel and, 162-167

P

Parker, Christopher, 95
Participant level of involvement, 166-167
Participative management, 144-146
Performance appraisal, rounded, 196-197
Personal relationships
    credibility paths based on, 103-109
    established over careers of managers, 90-91
    among key players, 67-68
    on OPMT Political Data Sheet, 68, 69
Pfeffer, Jeffrey, 53, 201
"Pickpocket's syndrome," 192
"Pike fish assumption," 22-24, 30, 47
Plan-Act Matrix, 168-174
Playing above board, 141-144, 149
Political activity, OPMT and indications of, 73
Political blind spot, 24, 27-51
    definition of, 27
    moral block and, 28-34, 108, 184
        manipulation versus influence and, 30-34
    rational block and, 34-41, 108
Political Data Sheet, OPMT, 64, 65, 68-69
Political savvy
    as an art form, xvi
    cautions regarding, 213-215
    characteristics of an individual with, 49
    Machiavellian characteristics versus, 44-47, 112
    definitions of, 111-113, 127-128, 204
    interests and, 43-44
    key challenges regarding, 213-217

Index

    as key dimension of leadership, xiv, 5-6
    natural, xiv-xv
    orientation, xvii
    political styles and, 22
    professional lobbying versus, 109-111
    steps to developing, 204-209
Political style(s), 7-24
    action orientation and, 9, 10-22
    Advisor, 11, 15, 22
    bias of various, 21
    conscious choice of, 22-24
    Cynic, 11, 12
    Fatalist, 11, 12-13, 22
    Leader, 11, 18-20, 22
    Machiavellian, 11, 16-17, 22
    political savvy and, 22
    Protector, 11, 14, 22
    Responsible, 11, 18, 22
    Spectator, 11, 13-14, 22
    Speculator, 11, 15, 22
    value orientation, 10-20
Political Style Grid, 10-11, 20, 23, 43
Political territory, mapping the. See Organization Politics
    Mapping Technique (OPMT)
Politics, negative view of, xv. *See also* Organization politics
Power coalitions and, 87-89
    of key players, 67
    need for, 28-30
    Savvy versus Mach view of, 46-47, 184
Predictable opposition forces, using, 186-188, 193-194
Prediction, political styles oriented toward, 11, 14-16
Prince, The (Machiavelli), 16
Processing, individual styles of, 157-158
Professional lobbying, political savvy versus, 109-111
Promotion system, 17-18
Protector style, 11, 14, 22

Q

Quinn, Robert E., 40-41

R

Rational block, 34-41, 108
Rational systems, organizations as, 36-37
Reports, special, 164
Resistance to change, 83-85, 129-130
Resources
    executive attention as strategic, 154-156, 179
    outside, OPMT for maximizing contributions of, 74
Respect for those in power, 46.
See also Credibility; Trust, executives' reliance on Responsible strategizing, 214
Resonsible style, 11, 18, 22
Risk
    Cynic style and, 12
    environment for taking, 171
    Spectator style and, 11, 13-14
    taking half-steps to diminish, 172
Rounded performance appraisal, 196-197

S

Sacrificial hit, taking the, 42
Sapolsky, Harvey, 115
Savvy, the. *See* Political savvy
Savvy attitude, 48-49
Self-destructive behavior, 43
Self-revelation, providing opportunities for Machiavellian's, 193-195
Single-issue lobbying, 111
"Skunk works" operations, 172
Snowflake Theory of strategic decisions, xvi
Special reports, use of, 164
Spectator style, 11, 13-14, 22
Speculator style, 11, 15, 22
Strategic resource, executive attention as, 154-156, 179
Strategy
    charting political. See Agenda linking
    giving priority to, over interpersonal skills, 111
    organization culture and implementation of, 119-124
    overstrategizing, risk of, 215-216
    responsible strategizing, 214

Index

Strategy level of coalition, 90-92
    brainstorming for win-win possibilities in, 99-101
    participant level of involvement in, 166-167
Style, political. See Political style(s)
Success
    leader style and, 19-20
    Responsible style and, 18
    seeing organization as human system and, 91
    See also Tactics
Systematic informality, 139-141, 149, 155, 156, 158, 164

T

Tabling, expert use of, 190
Tactics
    for building momentum, 128-150
    countering Machiavellian, 192-198
    in interpersonal diplomacy, 174-181
    See also Customizing influence
Task legitimization, coalitions and, 86
Teamwork, demonstration of, 176-177, 180
Technically oriented managers, 37
Timing, choosing right, 158-159
Tracy, Diane, 203
Trust, executives' reliance on, 159-160. *See also* Credibility
"Turf builders," 17-18
Two-shots-then-salute technique, 177-181

U

United States Constitution, 19
Unsavvy, the, xv
Urquart, Sir Brian, 35-36

V

Validity
    convergent, 85-86, 160-161, 195
    individual requirements for, 157-162
Value orientation toward political behavior, 10
    political style and, 10-22

on Political Style Grid, 10-11

W

Win-lose view, 12, 17, 175
Winning, gracious, 176-177
Win-win outcome, 19, 176
    brainstorming for, 99-101

X

X factor in OPMT, 75

Y

Yes-man syndrome, 178

Z

Zero inclusion, level of, 162